SCIENCE FOR GIRLS

SUCCESSFUL CLASSROOM STRATEGIES

Susan Gibbs Goetz

The Scarecrow Press, Inc.
Lanham, Maryland • Toronto • Plymouth, UK
2007

SCARECROW PRESS, INC.

Published in the United States of America
by Scarecrow Press, Inc.
A wholly owned subsidiary of
The Rowman & Littlefield Publishing Group, Inc.
4501 Forbes Boulevard, Suite 200, Lanham, Maryland 20706
www.scarecrowpress.com

Estover Road
Plymouth PL6 7PY
United Kingdom

British Library Cataloguing in Publication Information Available

Library of Congress Cataloging-in-Publication Data

Goetz, Susan Gibbs, 1945–
   Science for girls : successful classroom strategies / Susan Gibbs Goetz.
      p. cm.
   Includes bibliographical references and index.
   ISBN-13: 978-0-8108-5367-6 (pbk. : alk. paper)
   ISBN-10: 0-8108-5367-1 (pbk. : alk. paper)
   1. Science—Study and teaching. 2. Women—Education. I. Title.
Q181.G466 2007
507.1–dc22   2007020486

♾™ The paper used in this publication meets the minimum requirements of
American National Standard for Information Sciences—Permanence of Paper
for Printed Library Materials, ANSI/NISO Z39.48–1992.
Manufactured in the United States of America.

To Laura, Rebecca, Andrea, Erin, Jessica, Anna, and Allison—and to all my previous elementary- and middle-school students who were the inspiration for this book. I hope that our work together has had some positive effect on how you think about science today.

With thanks to Jay for his support and belief, to Linda Distad for encouraging me to put my work into book form, to the Education Department faculty at the College of St. Catherine for their continual support of all my work and for allowing me the time this project required, and to my previous and current college students—young women who have and will become strong, positive role models for girls in science education.

CONTENTS

1

GIRLS: UNIQUE FROM THE START

BRAIN-BASED RESEARCH

"Keep their minds, as much as you can, within common bounds, and teach them that their sex should feel a modesty with regard to science, almost as delicate as that which would inspire them with a horror of vice."[1] This quotation is taken from a book written in the nineteenth century and was chosen to introduce the subject of this book: science education for young women. As one can readily see from the quotation, science has not always been considered an appropriate subject for girls and women.

This chapter provides an overview of how girls learn by looking at what we currently think we know about brain development in the growing female. It will discuss why it is important that more of today's girls develop an interest in the sciences and careers in science and technology, and it will suggest how educators can support and encourage girls to pursue careers in science and technology. While the focus of the book is on science for girls, the implication is that by improving science education for girls, we are improving science education for all youngsters. This book is intended for all those interested in that pursuit.

GIRLS AND SCIENCE

A great deal of research indicates that not all girls achieve at the same level as boys in science and that they do not continue in these content areas into high school, or beyond in college and careers. Several studies confirm that as girls move through the educational system, their achievement and enrollment in science courses declines relative to those of boys. At age nine, girls and boys perform about the same on science assessments, except in the physical sciences. By around the age of thirteen, an achievement gap appears in most science content areas, and by age seventeen, girls achieve at a notably lower level than boys, particularly in physics. It is important to note that by age eleven, boys show a more positive view of science on interest surveys than girls do.[2]

Girls tend to drop out of the science "pipeline" sooner than boys. At the secondary level, girls select biology, but fewer girls, even high-achieving ones, opt for chemistry or physics compared to boys: "Of the students who take chemistry (an already limited segment of the school population), 34 percent are girls and 66 percent are boys; for physics the figures are 22 percent girls and 78 percent boys."[3]

The reasons for this disparity are related to both social pressures and science skills. We will look at the latest brain research as well as gender socialization at home and in schools as it influences girls' learning.

THE DEBATE

Males and females are equal in their common membership of the same species, humankind, but to maintain that they are the same in aptitude, skill, or behavior is to build a society based on a biological and scientific lie.[4]

The very fact that we are dealing with differences between boys and girls has led some researchers to link their search for causes to a biological category, sex. A child is born a boy or girl, and somehow that determines whether that child can become a better or worse mathematician. Yet research has failed to demonstrate any innate female inability to learn math and science. Biology cannot explain why such a large majority of women steer away from math- and science-related work."[5]

What are we to believe? According to SciMath Minnesota's "Best Practice * Science for All" (*K–12 Science Framework*, 2005),

Research has tended to focus on a *deficiency model* that identifies weaknesses and treats girls learning science as if they were the problem. This has led to considerations of how to make girls more aggressive, analytical, competitive, etc., or what one researcher has called "remedial masculinity." An *efficacy model* of what girls can do has shown that many of the "problems" lie in science classrooms as well as within out broader culture. There is *no* evidence that biological differences are responsible for the gender gap in science."[6]

HOW THE BRAIN WORKS

Regardless of what one believes about the issue discussed in the previous section, there are recent scientific findings about how the brain works. Following is some general information about brain functioning.

The human brain has approximately 100 billion neurons and 100 trillion *glial*, or connecting, cells. The three layers comprising the brain—the cerebral cortex at the top, the limbic system in the middle, and the brain stem at the bottom—weigh around eight pounds for an adult. The brain grows from the bottom up, beginning with the lower limbic system and brain stem, followed by the upper limbic system and the four lobes of the cerebral cortex, or *neocortex*.

Although the areas of the brain interact, the three layers carry out distinct functions. The brain stem is home of the fight-or-flight responses that we all know. Everyone has heard stories about superhuman feats performed during a crisis. The brain stem is the most primitive part of the brain and is responsible for this survival function.

In the middle of our brain is the limbic system, which processes emotion. Sensory stimuli enter the brain through the sense organs, and we experience emotions as a response to the stimuli. The amygdala, which lies at the bottom of the limbic system just above the brain stem, is sometimes responsible for aggressive responses, which are also generated in the brain stem.

Thinking occurs in the top of the brain in the four lobes of the neocortex. Different sensory stimulants are processed here, as well as in the limbic system. The neocortex handles most decision making. This area is divided into left and right hemispheres. The right hemisphere tends to be associated with verbal ability and communication, whereas the left hemisphere is associated primarily with spatial abilities, such as measuring, mechanical design, and perceiving direction.

When teaching content to a student, you work with the top portion of the brain unless the student demonstrates an emotional response to the assignment. In that case, the limbic system is interacting with the neocortex. Because the limbic system is a more primitive part of the brain, it slows down the cognitive thinking

Table 1.1. Developmental Gender Differences in Utero

Male	Female
Develops testosterone	Develops estrogen
Same structural brain first six weeks after conception	Same structural brain first six weeks after conception
"Set" *male* brain immune to *female* hormones	"Set" *female* brain immune to *male* hormones
Fetus generally more active, restless	Fetus generally less active in womb
Male cortex develops more slowly	*Female* cortex develops faster
At six weeks in utero sexual identity is determined, and brain changes	Normal template of human brain appears to be female
At six weeks colossal dose of male hormone changes brain permanently	Lack of testosterone impact allows brain structure to remain female
Brain is more lateral than female's	Brain is less lateral than male's
Less flexible	More flexible
Less internalized	Less externalized
Greater idling in brain stem (reptilian brain)	Greater idling in cingulate gyrus (limbic system)
Brain 10 percent larger (mass) than girl's	Brain mass 10 percent smaller in girls
Corpus callosum smaller	Corpus callosum larger
Produces less serotonin (quieting agent)	Produces more serotonin (quieting agent)

Source: *Boys and Girls Learn Differently!* by Michael Gurian; see also table 1.2.

in the neocortex. This is important when considering science education; if a girl thinks she is not capable of the work, she may indeed inhibit her own thinking. Brain research has shown that during an emotional crisis, blood flow is concentrated in the middle of the brain—the limbic system—and not in the neocortex, or thinking part of the brain.[7]

It is important to understand the basic workings of the human brain before looking at the similarities and differences in male and female brain functioning (see table 1.1). Although we all start as female in the womb, within a very short time changes occur to determine whether or not we will remain female or become male. The information in table 1.2, which was created by Michael Gurian,[8] outlines differences between males and females in utero and during infancy. This information is included because we would suspect that very few societal influences would occur at these levels. Indeed, in the uterus there cannot be any gender-related socialization taking place!

According to the work of Gurian, Howard Gardner, Robert Sylwester, and others, there are ten areas that brain-based research has been able to track over the course of the last two decades.[9] While this scientific progress is what we are seeing generally, it is important to state that there are many exceptions to all these findings.

Table 1.2. Developmental Gender Differences during Infancy

Male	Female
Prefers mechanical or structural toys	Prefers soft, cuddly toys
Looks at objects for shorter but more active periods	Plays with objects for longer periods, but less actively
Gazes at mother half as long as girl does	Play is more sanguine
Motor activity more vigorous than girl's	Motor activity less vigorous than boy's
At one week, cannot distinguish another baby's cry from background noise	At one week, able to distinguish another baby's cry from background noise
At four months cannot distinguish faces of people in photos	At four months able to recognize faces of people known in photos
Sensitive to salty foods	Sensitive to bitter tastes; prefers sweets
Less sensitive to physical sensation on skin	More sensitive to physical sensation on skin
More easily angered	More easily saddened
Better narrow vision and depth perception	Better peripheral vision
Superior perception at blue end of color spectrum	Superior perception at red end of color spectrum
Less attuned to sensory input than girls	More attuned to sensory input than boys

Source: *Boys and Girls Learn Differently!* by Michael Gurian; see also table 1.1.

Deductive and Inductive Reasoning. Girls tend to be inductive thinkers, beginning with a concrete example and building general theory. This reasoning style tends to occur earlier in the conceptualization process.

Abstract and Concrete Reasoning. Boys tend to be able to solve problems abstractly, or without seeing the problem, while girls tend to be more successful when given manipulatives and objects. Teaching mathematics on a blackboard, using signs and signifiers, may pose more difficulties for girls than would giving them tools to manipulate the problem.

Use of Language. On average, females produce more words than males. During the learning process (and in general), females use more words than males and use words as they learn while boys often work silently. This is also seen when observing students working in male-female groups. In addition, boys more often use jargon and coded language while girls prefer to conceptualize thinking with everyday words.

Logic and Evidence. Girls tend to be better listeners than boys and are more receptive in conversation to what has been said.

The Likelihood of Boredom. The fact that girls are better at self-managing boredom during instruction and all facets of education has a profound impact on all aspects of learning. When a child becomes bored, he or she may give up on learning and/or act out in such a way that class is disrupted and the child is labeled a behavioral problem.

Use of Space. Boys, particularly at younger ages, tend to occupy more space when playing or working in a classroom. This is seen when boys and girls work together: the boys tend to spread their work or toys into the girls' space.

Movement. Research has shown that girls move around less than boys while learning; however, movement breaks are helpful for both boys and girls at young ages.

Sensitivity and Group Dynamics. Girls function more successfully in cooperative groups than boys. Furthermore, girls seem to have a code of social interaction that assists them in group work. Interestingly, brain-based research has also shown that girls who may not be considered a "popular" member of the mainstream student population may also be less likely to fail in school than boys who are unpopular, not called on, or not socially assertive.

Use of Symbolism. Boys make more use of symbolic diagrams, graphs, and texts, particularly in the upper grades, while girls prefer written texts. This can be seen in literature classes where girls consider the emotions of the characters while boys are more interested in the author's symbolism.

Use of Learning Teams. The difference here is that boys tend to form structured teams while girls favor less structure.

SOCIALIZATION

We know that whether or not they think they do, adults begin very early in their children's lives to treat their children differently based on the child's sex.[10] In fact, this treatment begins even before birth. The sex of an unborn baby is the subject of much conversation; birth announcements are designed to indicate the child's sex; the sex is the first question asked by friends and family after the delivery, and the answer drives the gift giver's choice of clothing and accessory color. Furthermore, people's perceptions about the baby's size, attractiveness, and potential are determined by the baby's sex: "Girls are seen as smaller, softer, more fragile, weak and beautiful; boys as stronger, larger, more alert, coordinated, aggressive, and even athletic."[11]

Research I have conducted with my science methods students has provided anecdotal evidence that well-meaning parents as well as teachers discourage girls in the areas of science and math while encouraging them in the language arts. If we believe the brain research that indicates that girls are more successful in the verbal and communication area, then it is understandable that adults would praise girls in their areas of strength. In addition, the majority of adult students surveyed indicated they either have no memory of studying science at the elementary level or they remember learning science from a text-book. Teaching methodology might contribute to this perception: although professional scientists often need to work together to solve a problem, in the classroom, science is sometimes taught in an asocial manner, with students working individually. Science investigations, when assigned to students to complete individually, are rarely considered proper themes for essays, group discussions, or debate. Girls, who possess an interest in people and strong verbal skills, can be turned off to science at an early age when taught in this manner.

It should come as no surprise, then, that upon entering secondary school, where science courses become optional, many girls begin a downward spiral in enrollment, achievement, and interest in physical sciences: "The decline culminates in inadequate preparation for most college majors and vast under-representation of women in many mathematical, scientific, and technical fields of work—in some cases reaching a 99:1 ratio of men to women."[12]

According to Joan Skolnick's research, slightly more girls than boys are enrolled in school in the United States, yet twice as many college-bound senior boys as girls have taken three years of physical science. In a typical U.S. high school, boys outnumber girls by more than two to one in most physical science courses, and by three to one in physics.

The job market is a good place to look for the results of females' early science avoidance, which has resulted simultaneously in lower salaries for women and demand for women in higher-paying, science-related fields. Both single and married women are entering the job market in unprecedented numbers and staying longer; most women who work have an economic need to do so. In spite of the numbers, women continue to earn, on average, less than men who occupy the same positions. While social inequities are to blame for some of the poor earnings, the overwhelming majority of women workers are still concentrated in a relatively small number of lower-paying job categories while the job market progressively favors women with technical skills based on science and math preparation.[13]

In a 2002 article in the *Minneapolis Star Tribune*, Kate Rubin,[14] president of the Minnesota High Tech Association, congratulates the Twin Cities for rating as "the most competitive 'knowledge economy' in the world." She goes on, however, to state that "despite its glowing review, the survey fails to point out some of our state's weaknesses. For example, it doesn't explore whether we'll be able to supply companies with the educated workforce that will be required in coming decades."

According to Rubin, "Minnesota's top ranking is an acknowledgement of some of our state's core strengths—a well-educated workforce, relatively strong public education spending, and solid business investment in research. Unfortunately, unless action is taken soon, many of our state's future graduates may not have the math, science, or engineering skills required to sustain a strong knowledge economy. In a study issued earlier this year by the Minnesota High Tech Association, less than half of Minnesota's eighth-graders tested proficient in math and science."[15] Furthermore, because on average, boys score higher than girls on achievement tests, Rubin's findings are even more critical to the nature of science education for girls.[16]

Rubin's article goes on to look at global education standards. "As companies increasingly compete on a global scale, so too must communities that support such firms. Minnesota's K–12 education outperforms most other states, but we need to compare our region on an international level. According to the most recent figures from the Third International Mathematics and Science Study (TIMSS), fourth-graders in the United States rank 18th in science and 19th in math, well behind growing regions such as China and Singapore."[17]

Moreover, the Trends section in TIMSS data, disaggregated for gender, shows that girls tended to perform at about the same level as boys in life science, while boys were markedly stronger in earth science, physics, and chemistry.[18]

CONCLUSION

As a society, we cannot afford to inhibit the creativity of more than half our population. In these times of economic and environmental crisis, the quality and effectiveness of our social solutions depend on the perspectives that women, as well as men, bring to science and technology.

Several decades of changing sex-role awareness has taught us that what plagues one sex usually serves in one form or another to limit the full potential of the other sex. We stand to enrich the entire world of science by asking not why girls can't learn this subject, but why science isn't the sort of subject girls want to learn. In approaching our teaching of science in ways that encourage the intellectual styles and concerns of girls, we may bridge a gap between technical and social learning. That will benefit us all. In the process our efforts to understand what makes girls become anxious and avoid science will also help many boys with similar difficulties.

We as educators can take some steps to address the learning problems children develop. To increase girls' achievement in science, we must encourage the growth of intellectual self-confidence, develop problem-solving skills, and build on girls' verbal and interpersonal strengths in the learning process.

NOTES

1. Archbishop Fénelon, *The Education of a Daughter* (Bedford, MA: Applewood Books, 1847), 67.

2. Nancy Kober, "EDTALK: What Special Problems Do Girls Face in Science? What Can Schools and Teachers Do?" (Washington, DC: Council for Educational Development and Research), ERIC Documentation Reproduction Service No. ED361205.

3. Kober, "EDTALK."

4. Anne Moir and David Jessel, *Brain Sex* (New York: Dell, 1990), 11.

5. "SciMath Minnesota, K–12 Science Framework, Best Practice, Science for All," at www.scimathmn.org/frameworks_math.htm (accessed June 24, 2004).

6. "SciMath Minnesota, Best Practice, Science for All" (emphasis in the original).

7. Michael Gurian, *Boys and Girls Learn Differently!* (San Francisco: Jossey-Bass, 2001).

8. Chart from Gurian, *Boys and Girls Learn Differently!* 34–35.

9. Gurian, *Boys and Girls Learn Differently!*

10. Michael Lewis, "Parents and Children: Sex Role Development," *School Review* 80 (1972): 229–40.

11. Jeffrey Z. Rubin, Frank J. Provenzano, and Zella Luria, "The Eye of the Beholder: Parents' Views on Sex of Newborns," *American Journal of Orthopsychiatry* 44 (1974): 512–19.

12. Joan Skolnick, Carol Langbort, and Lucille Day, *How to Encourage Girls in Math and Science* (Palo Alto, CA: Dale Seymour Publications, 1982), 3.

13. Skolnick, Langbort, and Day, *How to Encourage Girls in Math and Science.*

14. Kate Rubin, "No Rest for the Best," *Minneapolis Star Tribune,* April 8, 2002, D3.

15. Rubin, "No Rest for the Best."

16. Rubin, "No Rest for the Best."

17. "TIMSS 1999 Benchmarking Report," at isc.bc.edu/timss1999b/sciencebench_report/t99bscience_chap_3_4.html.

18. "TIMSS 1999 Benchmarking Report."

2

GIRLS AND LEARNING: FALSEHOODS AND FACTS

LEARNING STYLES OF GIRLS

In January 2005, while still president of Harvard University, Larry Summers made some speculative comments about women's "intrinsic" abilities in science. Delivered during a presentation at a National Bureau of Economic Research (NBER) conference, his comments sparked a debate that put women and science in the spotlight, making it clear that the question no longer is whether women can succeed in the sciences, but how to encourage their success. The Summers dispute provides us with the opportunity to look closely at how girls learn, what their preferences and perspectives are regarding science, and how we can use this knowledge to attract girls to science and to boost public awareness of gender inequities. Moreover, the Summers controversy could lead to better opportunities for girls and incite excitement for science. (Summers's January 14, 2005, presentation, "Remarks at NBER Conference on Diversifying the Science & Engineering Workforce," appears online at www.president.harvard.edu/speeches/2005/nber.html. In addition, "Letter from President Summers on Women and Science," written in response to some of the criticism his speech prompted, appears at www.president.harvard.edu/speeches/2005/womensci.html.) Recognizing the differences in girls' and boys' learning styles prepares us to examine some of the research in this area.

RESEARCH ON CULTURALLY CONSTRUCTED GENDER DIFFERENCES

Babies experience their world by crawling, climbing, talking, touching, experimenting, taking chances, and building on their experiences, both positive and negative. Gender expectations help boys build trust in their ability to have some control over their environment, and girls may learn the value of closeness to adults for safety and security.[1] As reported in their book *How to Encourage Girls in Math and Science*,[2] Skolnick, Langbort, and Day found that parents

- "are more apprehensive about girls' well-being and protect them more;
- tend to direct boy babies away from their mothers starting at about six months, thus creating more opportunities for independent exploration, physical activity, and problem-solving;
- keep girls closer to home during play and assist them more in their activities; and encourage and maintain the close physical contact of early infancy for a longer time with daughters."[3]

Unless girls are encouraged to also challenge their environment with confidence, they will become fearful when the occasion to demonstrate independence arises. In one study, "girls were already showing signs of such dependency by thirteen months. Baby girls returned to the mothers more quickly and frequently when put down, and when a barrier was placed between mother and child, the girls became more upset and less aggressive in attempting to cross it."[4]

Studies of gender differences in the behavior of infants, toddlers, and young children lend evidence to adult stereotyping of newborns and treatment of preschoolers, and point to dependence training for girls. If schools, peers, and media reinforce these stereotypes and treatment, girls may grow to distrust their own abilities in unfamiliar skill areas like math and science.

In our society women continue to be the primary caretakers of infants and young children. As children grow and develop and enter formal school, many of their teachers are female. Therefore, as gender identification develops, girls learn to be "like mother" and "like teacher." Thus the young girl can imitate her role models and receive immediate feedback. As for boys, their differing process of gender identification presents different learning problems. Psychologist David Lynn indicates that in the gender-identification process boys accumulate practice at important kinds of problem solving and develop a learning style that involves primarily (1) defining the goal, (2) restructuring the situation, and (3) abstracting principles. The girls' task, on the other hand, involves learning the lesson as presented and promotes a style based more on personal relationship and imitation.[5]

This does *not* mean, however, that girls do not learn to abstract. As girls grow and develop, their abstract reasoning develops in a highly interpersonal context and focuses on different content—people and relationships. Consequently, girls may be less practiced at some kinds of analytic tasks used in math and science. Their social style of learning and interest in people-oriented content are not compatible with science *as girls are currently taught.*[6]

As educators we can take actions to address the learning problems children develop. To help girls succeed more in science, we must encourage girls' growth of intellectual self-confidence and the development of their problem-solving skills. We can build on girls' verbal and interpersonal strengths in the learning process. Science activities that are hands-on, involve group work and relevance, and include women role models are some of the strategies that we can use to build the confidence and problem-solving skills needed in the study of science.

In addition, research has shown that teachers' verbal behaviors influence what girls believe they can achieve.[7] In the science classroom, teachers have been observed to call on boys more often than girls and to use boys' names more frequently than girls' names. The result is differential encouragement of boys and girls based, perhaps, on the assumption that girls do not like science and/or it is not suitable for them. Teachers, therefore, should examine their behavior patterns to make sure they are equitable in terms of the ways they interact with boys and girls.

SciMath Minnesota has investigated strategies that are effective for increasing girls' interest and participation in science based on girls' learning styles and preferences. "Girls tend to be more interested than boys in topics that relate to people and their problems as well as to connecting . . . science to the everyday world."[8] The recommendation is to develop activities around the nature of science to show girls science's advantages and disadvantages to society and how to make value judgments surrounding what the students are learning in science.

SciMath also indicates that pairing girls with girls will provide equitable opportunities for them to use equipment.[9] This is important given that one study found that 79 percent of student-assisted science demonstrations were carried out by boys.[10]

RESEARCH ON GENDER DIFFERENCES IN PERSONALITY TRAITS ACROSS CULTURES

A report by the National Institutes of Health (NIH) found strong similarities in behavioral gender differences in a variety of geographical areas, including China, sub-Saharan Africa, Malaysia, India, the Philippines, In-

GIRLS AND LEARNING: FALSEHOODS AND FACTS

donesia, Peru, the United States, and Europe (including Croatia, the Netherlands, Belgium, France, Germany, Italy, Norway, Portugal, Spain, Yugoslavia, and western Russia). According to the authors, "Contrary to predictions from the social role model, gender differences were most pronounced in European and American cultures in which traditional sex roles are minimized."[11]

Other studies have illustrated differences in girls' and boys' approach to school. A meta-analysis by Alan Feingold indicated that psychologists have consistently found that girls tend to have higher standards in the classroom, and assess their own performance critically.[12] Furthermore, students' grades demonstrate that girls outperform boys in school in all subjects and grade levels. Because girls do better, one would imagine that they are more self-confident about their academic abilities and have higher self-esteem, but that does not seem to be the case. Rather, girls are more likely than boys to be critical in assessing their own academic performance. Interestingly, boys tend to have unrealistically high estimates of their abilities.[13] As a result, when a girl receives an A she feels she did not deserve it and that she was just lucky, but when a boy receives a B− he thinks he is quite intelligent. What this means to educators is that girls need a lot of encouragement (while boys may sometimes need a reality check!).

Educational psychologists have detected fundamental differences between the factors motivating girls and the factors motivating boys. Researchers have consistently found that "girls are more concerned than boys are with pleasing adults, such as parents and teachers."[14] On the other hand, boys are more motivated by material that interests them. The findings of Eva Pomerantz, Ellen Alterman, and Jill Saxon support these assertions:[15] "Girls generalize the meaning of their failures because they interpret them as indicating that they have disappointed adults, and thus they are of little worth. Boys, in contrast, appear to see their failures as relevant only to the specific subject area in which they have failed; this may be due to their relative lack of concern with pleasing adults. In addition, because girls view evaluative feedback as diagnostic of their abilities, failure may lead them to incorporate this information into their more general view of themselves. Boys, in contrast, may be relatively protected from such generalization because they see such feedback as limited in its diagnosticity."[16]

GENERAL CLASSROOM STRATEGIES FOR TEACHING SCIENCE TO GIRLS

"My students, future teachers, will impact the lives of girls and boys not yet born. I hope and trust that my female-friendly practices will extend to these classrooms of tomorrow."[17]

I have indicated that the material in this book is not intended for girls only. It is hoped that the strategies, lesson plans, and general information furnished here will help both girls and boys to increase their success in the science classroom. With that said, here are some general strategies for improving achievement in science based on what we currently know about the way girls learn.

Rice University's Equitable Classroom Practices Institute and Nancy Kober[18] have developed the following strategies that may be helpful.

Student-Teacher Interaction

- Hold all girls to high expectations for performance and provide them with active counseling and encouragement to counteract stereotypical messages.
- Call on girls as often as you do boys, and be sure to ask the girls some of the higher-level cognitive questions. Research shows that both male and female teachers initiate more interaction with boys, and on higher cognitive levels.
- Have high expectations of both male and female students. Do not encourage learned helplessness by overnurturing the girls.

9

- Educate teachers and other school staff to become aware of subtle behaviors that discourage girls or communicate low expectations.
- Encourage girls to be active learners by using manipulatives and providing hands-on learning experiences.
- Use gender-free language in classroom discourse.
- Use quality, precise feedback to girls' as well as boys' answers—not just a nod or a "good."
- Keep an interaction journal. Keep track of the quantity and quality of interactions with students.
- Make eye contact with all students and call them by name.
- Provide adequate wait time, perhaps three or five seconds, before calling on a student to answer the question. Girls often wait until they have formulated an answer before they raise their hands; boys often raise their hands immediately and then formulate an answer.
- Do not interrupt girls or let other students do so.
- Refrain from recruiting students to perform classroom "chores" based on traditional gender roles. Do not ask only boys to assist in carrying boxes and girls to clean the bookshelves.
- Be a model of unbiased behavior for not only your classroom, but the entire school.

Lesson Planning and Classroom Management

- Use abundant hands-on activities to counteract girls' lack of familiarity with physical science. Enlist girls to help in demonstrations and experiments.
- Mentally divide your room into quadrants. If students in all quadrants do not participate, you can say, "Let's hear from someone in the back right corner."
- Balance cooperative and competitive activities. Research shows that most girls learn more readily in cooperative situations.
- Establish rules for participation and rotate jobs within each group.
- Give girls an equal amount of assistance and feedback. Boys usually receive more help and praise that builds self-esteem.
- Ask students to discuss concepts orally. This helps them learn the vocabulary of the subject.
- Encourage all students to take additional math and science courses. Adult encouragement proves to be a major factor in students' decision-making processes.
- Encourage girls to participate in extracurricular math and science activities. Some schools have organized girls' clubs where female students interact with mentors in the fields of math, science, technology, and engineering.
- Sponsor a girls' technology club. Plan activities that use technology in real-life scenarios. (Do the same for math and science.)
- Provide opportunities for female students to teach lessons or tutor younger students or even parents in math, science, and technology. As a teacher, you will ascertain that the girls really know the content. Furthermore, the opportunity to verbalize knowledge fosters higher self-esteem.
- Stress safety precautions instead of dangers. Girls will sometimes be reluctant to participate in lab activities that seem too dangerous.
- Insist that girls as well as boys learn to set up and use all electronic equipment: VCRs, video and digital cameras, printers, scanners, DVD players, etc.
- Address inappropriate behavior with a fair and respectful attitude, regardless of students' gender, race, ethnicity, or socioeconomic class. Videotape yourself to monitor your actions.
- Structure science activities so that girls play active rather than passive roles; take special steps to ensure that boys do not dominate lessons.

- Use computer and lab partners. Again, most girls work better in cooperative groups or on teams.
- Introduce lessons with an overview. Females learn more readily from the "big picture" than from disconnected details.
- Provide female role models. Research shows that girls need to see females in certain professions or career choices to visualize themselves in the same or similar roles, whereas boys need only to hear about certain roles to imagine themselves in those same roles.
- Provide learning experiences for girls to develop spatial visualization skills.
- Provide plenty of opportunities for cooperative learning, which can improve instruction for both girls and boys.
- Use writing to help students express and clarify their feelings and thoughts (e.g., math autobiographies, science journals).
- Create an attractive classroom environment. Research shows that girls learn better in an aesthetically pleasing environment.
- To appeal to students with various learning styles, encourage students to solve problems by using multiple methods.
- Encourage guessing, questioning, and exploration to reduce girls' anxiety and build their confidence about science.

Curriculum Content

- Use gender-inclusive language.
- Avoid generalizations that stereotype women in certain roles.
- Encourage a can-do attitude; teach students to give themselves credit. Females tend to credit their achievements to luck rather than to their abilities.
- Analyze curricular materials for bias. Supplement as needed.
- Take girls to an Expanding Your Horizons conference in your area. These conferences, sponsored by the American Association of University Women (AAUW), provide girls with access to workshops led by female professionals in the areas of math, science, technology, and engineering.
- Use toys to teach concepts in math and science. Traditionally, toys that cultivate understanding of math and science concepts are typically marketed as "boys' toys."
- Set aside an area in the classroom to serve as a resource center that contains materials about career opportunities in math, science, technology, and engineering.
- Diversify classroom resources to include females and diverse races.
- Celebrate Women's History Month.
- Assign biographical essays to students. Focus on male and female inventors and females in other areas of math, science, and technology.
- Acknowledge the contributions of both men and women to mathematics and science via posters, reports, examples, story problems, and so on.
- Showcase female role models and career options by bringing in guest scientists, disseminating career information, and creating bulletin boards about women in science.
- Discuss current events that are representative of women and other minorities with varying economic, legal, and social concerns.
- Invite guest speakers of both genders to speak to students.
- Incorporate students' comments into lectures. This technique validates the students' understanding of concepts.
- Use gender-fair books and materials.

- Help female students value themselves. Girls often experience severe drop in self-esteem during the middle-school years. Female teachers need to model a healthy self-respect and male teachers need to have respect for both girl students and female colleagues.

CONCLUSION

As previously stated, this book does not attempt to determine the reason for the science gender gap. There is a great deal of research on the workings of the brain that has shown that the female and male brains function differently, but we cannot say definitively that brain differences cause differences in how boys and girls learn science. We also know that culture and socialization play a role in how boys and girls perceive science. The most critical question, then, is what schools and teachers can do to reverse this situation. Fortunately, recent research is replete with recommendations for classroom activities that empower girls in science. This chapter concludes with general classroom strategies for effectively teaching science to girls.

NOTES

1. Joan Skolnick, Carol Langbort, and Lucille Day, *How to Encourage Girls in Math and Science* (Palo Alto, CA: Dale Seymour Publications, 1982).
2. Skolnick, Langbort, and Day, *How to Encourage Girls.*
3. Skolnick, Langbort, and Day, *How to Encourage Girls*, 14–15.
4. Skolnick, Langbort, and Day, *How to Encourage Girls*, 14.
5. Skolnick, Langbort, and Day, *How to Encourage Girls.*
6. Skolnick, Langbort, and Day, *How to Encourage Girls.*
7. "SciMath Minnesota, K–12 Science Framework, Best Practice, Science for All," at www.scimathmn.org/frameworks_math.htm (accessed June 24, 2004).
8. "SciMath Minnesota, Best Practice, Science for All."
9. "SciMath Minnesota, Best Practice, Science for All."
10. Nancy Kober, "EDTALK: What Special Problems Do Girls Face in Science? What Can Schools and Teachers Do?" (Washington, DC: Council for Educational Development and Research), ERIC Documentation Reproduction Service No. ED361205.
11. Paul Costa, Antonio Terracciano, and Robert McCrae, "Gender Differences in Personality Traits Across Cultures: Robust and Surprising Findings," *Journal of Personality and Social Psychology* 81, no. 2 (2001): 322–31.
12. Alan Feingold, "Gender Differences in Personality: A Meta-Analysis," *Psychological Bulletin* 116 (1994): 429–56.
13. Eva Pomerantz, Ellen Alterman, and Jill Saxon, "Making the Grade but Feeling Distressed: Gender Differences in Academic Performance and Internal Distress," *Journal of Educational Psychology* 94, no. 2 (2002): 396–404.
14. Pomerantz, Alterman, and Saxon, "Making the Grade," 397.
15. Pomerantz, Alterman, and Saxon, "Making the Grade," 402.
16. Pomerantz, Alterman, and Saxon, "Making the Grade," 402.
17. Jody Bart, *Women Succeeding in the Sciences* (West Lafayette, IN: Purdue University Press, 2000), 106.
18. Kober, "EDTALK."

TURNING GIRLS ON TO SCIENCE

SCHOOLS TODAY

One of the requirements I have for my students in Elementary Science Methods is to spend time in the field observing science lessons as they are taught. The students are required to observe at least two science lessons at the elementary level. The following is an e-mail message I received recently from one of my students:

> "Please find my fieldwork logs attached. I had a difficult time finding science classes to observe. Timing played a large factor in this, but also the lack of science being taught in the early elementary grades was a factor. My third-grade daughter has yet to have a science lesson and we are now into December! This is disturbing!
>
> "The teacher that I was able to connect with was superb. She expressed dismay at having to cut back from having science class three times a week to two times a week this year. The district has told the teachers that reading and math are the top priorities and if anything needs to be cut, science is one of those things. The district's logic is that the students will have science in middle school. What a shame! I hope this philosophy changes soon."[1]

This student's complaint is not unusual. The preservice education majors tell me that science at the elementary level, if it is taught at all, is taught perhaps twice a week. While this book was written to address science strategies for girls, it should be noted that neglecting to offer science classes, or putting them on the back burner, transmits another subtle message to our girls—science is just not important.

Focusing on the elementary level, this chapter provides the reader with a brief background of science education in today's schools.

DECLINING INTEREST IN SCIENCE EDUCATION

In the mid-1980s, a "crisis" was declared in science education. National assessments indicated there was a major problem in science education in elementary and secondary schools:[2] the studies revealed a decline in achievement and interest in science. Moreover, the National Assessment of Educational Progress (NAEP) uncovered a lack in understanding of basic science concepts.[3] Many high-school graduates and some college students could not apply their science knowledge to real-life situations.[4,5] Reports on international comparisons of student assessments also revealed that American students did not measure up to students in other developed countries in science and mathematics.[6,7,8] The educational system appeared to be failing in its task of preparing students for responsible citizenship and productive employment. Consequently, there was a national outcry for reform in science, mathematics, and technology education.

The American Association for the Advancement of Science (AAAS) responded to this outcry by launching a comprehensive, long-term reform effort, Project 2061. This project proposed a fundamental reform of science education focused on achieving scientific literacy for all Americans. Two documents were produced: *Science for All Americans*,[9] which defined scientific literacy, and *Benchmarks for Scientific Literacy*,[10] which served as a blueprint on which individual states are building science standards. Various groups working on science reform at the state and national levels still use both documents.

Today, basic knowledge of science is viewed as important for all citizens to have in order to participate effectively in a highly scientific and advanced technological society.[11] We would hope that a major goal of science education today would be science literacy for all Americans. There is evidence that financial and human resources are being used all over the United States to restructure and redesign K–12 science education. New programs are being designed and implemented and states are busy developing science standards at the elementary-, middle-, and high-school levels.

Following the publication of *Science for All Americans*,[12] the National Research Council (NRC) coordinated the development of national science education standards. These standards describe what students should understand and be able to do at different grade levels and in various content areas of science.

According to the *National Science Education Standards*, "The real journey of educational reform and the consequent improvement of scientific literacy *begin* with the implementation of these standards."[13] Defining scientific literacy and mapping out what it means to be scientifically literate are only the beginning of a long trek through the reform process. The most difficult task in an education reform effort of this nature is implementation. There is initially an urgent need to provide teachers with professional-development experiences that will enable them to apply the new standards. Then, teacher-education institutions need to provide learning experiences within their programs that will effectively prepare beginning teachers to put the new standards in place.

An example of successful professional development can be found in a law passed by the Missouri Legislature in 1993.[14] Along with several new programs and policies, the law called for the establishment of academic performance standards that all students should obtain before graduating from high school. The standards would then serve as a basis for a revised statewide testing program and a guide for school curriculum. Within the context of this law, reform in science education was initiated and new science standards and curriculum frameworks were developed.[15] Southwest Missouri State University created a teacher-enhancement project, funded by Missouri's Higher Education Eisenhower Grant Program, to provide professional-development experiences that would enable teachers to implement the national and state standards.[16] The project consisted of weekend workshops totaling sixty hours of instruction. Workshops focused on the content of the reform documents (science content standards, science teaching standards, assessment standards, and science program standards), hands-on activities, inquiry, discussion, and development of curriculum materials. The workshops were spread out through the year to give teachers enough time to reflect on new knowledge, practice new skills, and try out new ideas. At the end of the academic year, a variety of assessment and evaluation procedures were used to determine the effectiveness of the workshops. These included surveys, classroom observations, interviews, journals, and continuous assessment of group products and individual tasks throughout the workshops. All the evidence obtained from the various evaluation methods indicates that teachers have been making every effort to implement the knowledge, skills, techniques, and strategies that they learned in the workshops.[17]

What have we learned from this project? This experience and others like it show us that a change in teacher behavior can occur when teachers see that the reform is necessary, and then acquire the knowledge and skill sets needed. Teachers in the project described above became familiar with teaching and learning standards outlined by the reform movement, and reflected on their own teaching and science programs with reference to the new standards. Teachers in the project took the reform efforts into their own schools and districts, thus serving as change agents. It is a given that change in education does not occur overnight. However, with professional-development opportunities like the Missouri project, perhaps we can hope for long-term success in science education reform.

TODAY'S SCIENCE EDUCATION TRAINING PROGRAMS AND CLASSROOM PRACTICES

"People often ask me, 'If we can send a man to the moon, why can't our students achieve in science?'" This statement was made by Dr. Mae C. Jemison, the nation's first African American astronaut and national spokesperson for Making Science Making Sense (MSMS).[18] The response reported by the Bayer Corporation, which in 2004 conducted a survey of deans of teacher-training colleges and new teachers, is, "Because we haven't made it a priority." The survey asked an additional question: "How can we expect our students to achieve in science when the message to their teachers is that science is less important for them, too?"[19] The study went one step further, asking: "If teachers do not consider science important, how can we expect our girls to become interested and achieve in science?"

Ten years after the National Research Council's publication of the *National Science Education Standards*, a survey commissioned by Bayer Corporation as part of its MSMS program indicated that "elementary school science still remains a second-tier subject, both in teacher training and in today's classrooms."[20]

According to the Bayer survey, deans at the nation's colleges and universities who are responsible for training the newest elementary-school teachers indicate that science education should be given the same attention as reading, writing, and math at the elementary level. And while the deans evidently recognize the importance of science education, they are not confident that their own graduating teachers' qualifications to teach K–5 science are on par with their ability to teach reading, writing, and social studies. In order to provide a progress report on science education, the survey polled deans of education as well as K–5 schoolteachers with three to five years of experience. The survey reveals a "consistent message that says science in our schools is considered less important than reading, writing, and math—a message that is seen in college/university elementary education programs and subsequently carried over to teaching in classrooms across the country."

The survey consisted of a series of questions about the deans' and teachers' preservice training programs. Among one of the most significant findings is that science is cited by the most teachers (63 percent) as the subject they wish had been given more emphasis during their preservice training. And both deans (84 percent) and teachers (72 percent) agree that "elementary teacher education programs should require their undergraduates to take more coursework both in science itself and in science teaching methods."[21] A few more statistics are applicable here:

- Almost all teachers reported teaching reading and writing (95 percent) every day while one-third said they teach science every day (35 percent).
- Just over one-third (38 percent) of the teachers said they lack full confidence in their qualifications to teach science.
- Almost one-third (30 percent) assigned a grade of C or D to their school's science education program, with only 14 percent rating the science program an A.

The survey was not all gloom and doom, however. Findings showed that progress is being made in moving to inquiry-based science teaching methods. A majority of deans (74 percent) indicated the National Science Education Standards have had an impact on their institutions' teacher-education programs. Both deans and teachers (95 percent and 93 percent respectively) agreed that discussion and hands-on experiments and activities are effective teaching techniques. And 78 percent of new teachers indicated they are now using inquiry-based science instruction "most often" in their classrooms.

While the Bayer report is optimistic that movement is in the right direction, it is obvious that K–5 science education continues to need a stronger emphasis at the preservice level. There are examples of colleges and universities that have developed programs that provide inquiry-based science content and methodology. A few of these—the College of St. Catherine (St. Kate's), an all-women's private college in St. Paul, Minnesota; Simmons College, another all-women's private college in Boston; Tufts University, in suburban Boston; and the University of Kentucky in Lexington—are described below.

The College of St. Catherine has devised a program called STEM (Science, Technology, Engineering and Mathematics), a minor designed for elementary teacher candidates. The program consists of five four-credit courses that are team-taught by one science and one education faculty member. Courses are interdisciplinary in the science, technology, engineering, and mathematics content areas.

St. Kate's also does outreach work. On Saturday, March 5, 2005, nearly two hundred junior-high- and high-school-aged girls gathered with their parents at St. Kate's for Science Saturday, a program sponsored by the college's Center for Women, Science and Technology (CWST). Science Saturday is an event designed to engender interest among young women in the math, science, and technology fields. This unadvertised event was so popular that there was a waiting list of eager participants. St. Kate's expanded the event in 2007 to accommodate a larger group.

Also in March 2005, 170 middle-school-aged girls went to Simmons College for a science and technology conference run by the Girls Get Connected Collaborative. Activities included dissecting a sheep's brain and assembling dismantled computers. Girls also got referrals to the collaborative's summer and after-school programs. The focus was on middle school, the level at which research suggests that girls' interest in science wanes. Deborah Muscella, the organizer of the conference, hopes greater awareness will lead to more funding and future similar opportunities.

In the same month, two hundred Girls Scouts attended a workshop at Tufts University run by the Boston section of the Society of Women Engineers. The girls learned about plastic, electrical, mechanical, civil, and chemical engineering and about the history of women engineers.

The University of Kentucky, with funding from the federal government, sponsors Girls in Science, a program for middle-school girls that aims to convince them to pursue careers in math, science, engineering, and technology. The program challenges students with hands-on experiments in Saturday sessions at southeastern Kentucky colleges.

DRAW A SCIENCE TEACHER

According to a paper by Thomas and Pedersen presented at the April 1999 Boston conference of the National Association for Research in Science Teaching Conference, "Research literature indicates elementary school science is taught much as it always has been."[22] These researchers found that science classrooms do not change and science methods courses have changed little in spite of national reform movements and empirical research about the value of hands-on learning and inquiry teaching and learning. Thomas and Pedersen ask if it is possible "that a long history of stereotypical science learning experiences—in elementary school, high school, and college—powerfully impact the way in which elementary teachers understand the nature of science and the way in which science should be taught."[23] In other words, is it possible that preservice teachers bring earlier images and beliefs from their own experiences as students of science to the science methods courses? The Draw-A-Science-Teacher Test (DASTT-C) checklist may provide some insights.

The DASST-C extracts students' perceptions about themselves as science teachers. Simply put, the study compares illustrations of science teachers by elementary-school children and elementary preservice teachers, reviews science autobiographies of elementary preservice teachers, and considers the way early science learning experiences contribute to the basic understandings of elementary science teaching methods. This research indicates that as early as third grade, children begin to develop a stereotypical view of teaching science, and their perceptions closely match those of elementary preservice teachers. The autobiographies further describe earlier school experiences that match the elementary preservice teachers' illustrations.[24]

The children in the study came from a variety of backgrounds and classroom experiences, some of which included experience with Full Option Science System (FOSS), Activities Integrating Mathematics and Science (AIMS), and Project Wild curriculum materials—all of which utilize inquiry and discovery in their approach to the teaching of science. Overall, the DASTT-C data indicated that most of the students in the study (grades 3–11) drew pictures of the teacher giving directions or talking at the overhead projector or chalkboard while children were sitting in rows or groups. In other words, they put the teacher at the center of the learning. The autobiographies indicated that preservice teachers remember significant events and people, such as science fairs, field trips, and specific teachers (both positive and negative). Comments made included statements that science is "hard" and science is for boys, and self-deprecating comments about the individual's not being smart enough to do well in science. The positive or "good" teachers remembered in the autobiographies were those who encouraged hands-on activities and discussion while the "bad" teachers lectured and taught from the textbook.[25]

Research conducted with my own students confirms these findings. When I have asked my preservice science methods students to draw a science teacher on the first day of my class, the majority (71 percent) have drawn a male teacher wearing glasses (90 percent), either sitting or standing at a chalkboard (57 percent). In some instances the male science teacher was bald (19 percent) and wore "outlandish" (e.g., checkered pants) clothes (43 percent), which I have interpreted as the science teacher's having a geeky or nerdy persona. Keep in mind that I teach at an all-women's college, and that my students are studying to become elementary teachers who will be (we hope!) teaching science.

The research conducted by Thomas and Pedersen indicates that the pictures drawn by children and elementary preservice teachers were similar. There were differences in sophistication, but they were basically the same in terms of room arrangements, teacher positions, and student participation. Findings confirm the theory that earlier experiences in science education shape the way in which preservice teachers perceive the teaching of science. Thomas and Pedersen ask, Given that beliefs and expectations are formed at such a young age, what science pedagogy methods can professors and staff developers ever hope to teach? The authors suggest that simply using the DASTT-C with preservice teachers and pointing out the findings and implications can in itself help students discover their own prior understandings and how these shape their current beliefs about science teaching. Thomas and Pedersen suggest that "the more preservice teachers understand the influence of their own science learning experiences, the more methods professors can assist their professional development."[26]

NO CHILD LEFT BEHIND ACT

The No Child Left Behind Act (NCLB), instituted by President George W. Bush's administration, has had an effect across the nation as schools and districts work to improve students' understanding and achievement in math and reading and as teachers work to demonstrate that they are "highly qualified" in their areas of specialization. Schools are evaluated according to their adequate yearly progress (AYP), which is the primary measure of success or failure under the law. Sanctions for not achieving AYP include offering students a choice of schools to attend or restructuring the school. Due to the nature of the tests, there are countless sources indicating that since 2004, efforts to improve annual test scores in reading and mathematics in grades 3–8 have pushed aside science teaching. But now science is gaining importance as schools prepare for testing in 2007–2008, although the results of science tests will not be counted as a factor in whether schools make AYP unless states decide to voluntarily use the scores. The National Science Teachers Association (NSTA) recently conducted an informal survey of state science supervisors and found that very few states were considering including science test scores in the AYP at this time.[27] This situation implies that although states are beginning to think about science instruction again, the emphasis will continue to be on math and language arts.

The pressure on teachers to demonstrate that they are "highly qualified" in the subject they teach has affected science instruction primarily at the secondary level, where in some instances, teachers are assigned positions outside their fields because of budgetary limitations and staffing needs. The content area most in need of "fixing" is physics, according to Bill Robertson, author of several books published by the NSTA and a former curriculum director who conducts workshops for science teachers sponsored by the NSTA. His workshops focus on helping science teachers improve their core understanding of science concepts.[28] Robertson believes that today's science teachers have had inadequate science instruction, receiving too much complex material in too short a time at the expense of mastering core content.

GOOD NEWS AND BAD NEWS

Several reports indicate that more girls than boys are now enrolling in science courses at the secondary level.[29] However, girls continue to underenroll in physics and chemistry; these are the areas that provide high-paying careers for young adults entering the workforce.

Another indication that science is beginning to matter is that in 2004 the U.S. Department of Education and the National Science Foundation called the first ever science summit, which focused on the need to improve science education in the nation. The one-day event was part of a larger Excellence in Science, Technology, and Mathematics Education Week, also sponsored by these groups, to support math and science education.[30] The summit included the release of a national survey on parents' attitudes toward science education. The survey indicated that the majority of parents (94 percent) feel that science education is "very important." More than half (51 percent) indicated they believed they had more science when they were in school than their children are receiving. This can be interpreted to mean that parents feel science is important, but that their children are not getting a sufficient amount of science instruction.

CONCLUSION

This chapter has focused on science instruction in today's classrooms. While findings are not specific to science education for girls, we can conclude that if science instruction in general is lacking or insufficient for all children, it may be having twice the negative effect on our girls. The preceding chapters have demonstrated that girls are not encouraged to take an interest in science, that girls lack confidence in science classes, and that both interest and achievement begin to wane as early as third and fourth grade. If this is compounded by poor instruction, the result can be only what we are seeing: girls who become women who shy away from science and science careers. The number of science teachers who feel inadequate to teach science at the elementary level only compounds this situation. There appears to be a cycle of failure that needs to be broken by more comprehensive preservice science instruction for our future teachers, and science taught in our elementary schools that is geared towards girls' learning styles—hands-on, inquiry based, and discussion based. Because these are techniques that have proved successful for all children, both boys and girls will win if these methods are utilized.

The latter part of this book will focus on science activities that align with the learning styles of girls and what we know about brain research that can be used successfully in the heterogeneous elementary- and middle-school classroom.

NOTES

1. J. O. Harmon, e-mail message to author, December 2004.

2. Ernest Boyer. *High School: A Report on Secondary Education in America* (New York: Harper & Row, 1983).

3. National Assessment of Educational Progress (NAEP), *The Third Assessment of Science, 1981–1982* (Denver, CO: 1983).

4. Audrey Champagne and Leo Klopfer, "Research in Science Education: The Cognitive Psychology Perspective," in *Research Within Reach: Science Education*, ed. David Holdzkom and Pamela B. Lutz (Charleston, WV: Research and Development Interpretive Service, Appalachia Educational Laboratory, 1984), 172–89.

5. Robert Yager and John Penick, "Resolving the Crisis in Science Education: Understanding Before Resolution," *Science Education* 71, no. 1 (1987): 49–55.

6. International Association for the Evaluation of Educational Achievement, *Science Achievement in Seven Countries: A Preliminary Report* (Oxford: Pergamon, 1988).

7. Margrete Klein and F. James Rutherford, ed., *Science Education in Global Perspective: Lessons from Five Countries* (Boulder, CO: Westview Press, 1985).

8. Archie Lapointe, Nancy Mead, and Gary Phillips, *A World of Differences: An International Assessment of Mathematics and Science* (Princeton, NJ: National Assessment of Educational Progress, Educational Testing Service, 1989).

9. F. James Rutherford and Andrew Ahlgren, *Science for All Americans* (New York: Oxford University Press, 1990).

10. American Association for the Advancement of Science, *Benchmarks for Scientific Literacy* (New York: Oxford University Press, 1993).

11. Farella L. Shaka, "Translating Current Science Education Reform Efforts into Classroom Practices" (paper, Association for the Education of Teachers of Science conference, 1997), at www.ed.psu.edu/ci/Journals/97pap6.htm.

12. Rutherford and Ahlgren, *Science for All Americans*.

13. National Research Council, *National Science Education Standards (Update)* (Washington, DC: National Academy Press, 1995), 243.

14. Department of Elementary and Secondary Education, *The Outstanding Schools Act: Senate Bill 380*, Jefferson City, MO, 1993.

15. Shaka, "Translating."

16. Department of Elementary and Secondary Education, *Missouri's Proposed Academic Performance Standards (Draft)*, Jefferson City, MO, 1994.

17. Shaka, "Translating."

18. "Bayer Facts of Science Education Survey, 2004," at www.bayerus.com/MSMS/news/facts.cfm?mode=detail&id=survey04.

19. "Bayer Facts."

20. "Bayer Facts."

21. "Bayer Facts."

22. Julie A. Thomas and Jon E. Pedersen, "When Do Science Teachers Learn to Teach? A Comparison of School Children's and Pre-Service Teachers' Science Teacher Illustrations" (paper, conference of the Association for the Education of Teachers of Science, 2001), at www2.tltc.ttu.edu/thomas/conference%20paper/2001/2001.htm

23. Julie A. Thomas and Jon E. Pedersen, "Draw-a-Science-Teacher-Test: Pre-service Elementary Teachers Perceptions of Classroom Experiences" (paper, meeting of the National Association of Researchers in Science Teaching, San Diego, CA, April 1998).

24. Thomas and Pedersen, "Draw-a Science-Teacher-Test."

25. Thomas and Pedersen, "Draw-a-Science-Teacher-Test."

26. Thomas and Pedersen, "Draw-a-Science-Teacher-Test."

27. Sean Cavanagh, "As Test Date Looms, Educators Renewing Emphasis on Science," *Education Week*, March 30, 2005.

28. Sean Cavanagh, "Faking It Won't Make It in Science," *Education Week*, December 1, 2004.

29. Public Policy Institute of California, "High School Girls Now Outnumber Boys in Most Math and Science Classes," press release, March 5, 2005.

30. Michelle Galley, "Studies Suggest Science Education Neglected," *Education Week*, May 19, 2004.

4

STRATEGIZE FOR SUCCESS
Effective Strategies in Teaching Science

This chapter first looks at best practices in teaching science, as recommended by several national organizations. There then follows a variety of lesson plan styles that align with girls' learning styles. A list of resources is included as well. Suggested activities can be delivered using the lesson plan format that best suits the students' learning styles. These strategies and activities will also engage boys in learning science.

The following section is taken from *Keeping America Competitive: Five Strategies to Improve Math and Science Education*, by Charles Coble and Michael Allen.[1]

FIVE STRATEGIES

The Education Commission for the States and the National Science Foundation recently gathered experts in mathematics and science education in order to identify a variety of areas that policymakers and education leaders should address to improve mathematics and science education. Of particular importance are the needs to:

- Effectively access student learning in math and science
- Strengthen teacher knowledge and skills in math and science
- Ensure that high-quality math and science teachers are available to the most disadvantaged students
- Ensure strong leadership from the higher-education community, especially from university presidents
- Promote public awareness of the importance of math and science education in the country's future

The needs list does not end there. Below are five strategies that incorporate the pressing needs for improved research into a more comprehensive approach for improving mathematics and science education. As part of this comprehensive approach, the strategies are targeted toward a large audience, including policymakers, education leaders, the higher-education community, and the public at large.

Strengthen Math and Science Assessments

- The National Science and Mathematics Standards should be analyzed to find those core elements that student assessments might be linked around.
- The National Science and Mathematics Standards should be used to make appropriate changes to textbook and curriculum materials.

- Tests must be developed to measure both subject knowledge and overall student understanding of math and science concepts.

Ensure that Teachers Have Adequate Knowledge and Skills

- Education leaders and schools of education must draw on the nearly two decades of research addressing the knowledge and skills needed to teach math effectively.
- Researchers and policymakers should work to develop more studies on the knowledge and skills needed to teach science effectively.
- Research findings should be used to revise and improve teacher education, training, and professional-development programs.

Refer to appendix A for a description of the 2006 conference that was presented by the Center for Women, Science and Technology at the College of St. Catherine. The conference, "Why the Difference?" focused on best practices for building skills in teaching K–12 science, technology, engineering, and math.

Give the Neediest Students the Best Teachers

- Offer higher pay for math and science teachers who serve in hard-to-staff schools.
- Provide strong mentoring and induction programs for all new teachers.
- Develop cross-district programs that encourage experienced teachers to teach for several years in an urban district without loss of their seniority, pension, or pay privileges if they return to their original district.
- Develop accommodations with teacher unions that promote incentives for math and science teachers to work in hard-to-staff schools.

Enlist the Entire School in the Effort to Improve Teacher Education

- Ensure that original research is connected to what policymakers need. Compensation, tenure, and career-advancement incentives should be given to researchers whose work is most useful to policymakers.
- Identify promising ways of attracting talented students to become math and science teachers.
- Connect more math and science teachers with university researchers.
- Make it clear that the responsibility for preparing teachers rests not with the school of education, but with the institution as a whole—especially the arts and sciences faculty.
- Ensure that graduates of education programs are supported, mentored, and tracked over time.
- Review teacher-education programs, focusing on:
  - The extent to which prospective teachers are grounded in the academic content area in which they will teach, proven practical teaching skills, and using technology in the classroom
  - The quality of students admitted to the program. Admission and performance standards for students in teacher-education programs should match or exceed those of the student body as a whole
  - The steps that teacher education programs are taking to attract and retain talented minority students

Engage the Greater Public

- Develop a series of clear messages that resonate with the public and with policymakers on the need to improve mathematics and science education.

- Engage communications specialists to translate research findings into materials that resonate with the public, policymakers, parents, and young people who may choose to become tomorrow's math and science teachers.
- Engage the business community in sending an urgent message to policymakers and the public of the importance of math and science education to the U.S. economy.
- Engage university presidents and educators as visible, vocal advocates for improving math and science education at all levels.

NATIONAL SCIENCE EDUCATION STANDARDS

We next turn our attention to what the current research tells us is the "best" science education for all of our children. Today's trend in all content areas is to look at our goals and outcomes first—what we want children to know and be able to do—and then plan assessment, teaching, and learning around those objectives. Most states and school districts within the states have developed science standards that use the National Science Education Standards (NSES) as their framework. The NSES are designed to improve science education for all students regardless of gender and are therefore devoid of reference to girls or boys. The sections below are taken from the 1996 National Science Education Standards,[2] which support the tenets of this book.

Developing Student Abilities and Understanding, Grades K–4

From the earliest grades, students should experience science in a form that engages them in the active construction of ideas and explanations that enhance their opportunities to develop the ability to do science. Teaching science as inquiry allows teachers to develop student abilities and to enrich student understanding of science. Students should do science in ways that suit their developmental capabilities.

In the early years of school, students can investigate earth materials, organisms, and properties of common objects. Although children develop concepts and vocabulary from such experiences, they also should develop inquiry skills. As students focus on the processes involved in doing investigations, they develop the ability to ask scientific questions, investigate aspects of the world around them, and use their observations to construct reasonable explanations for the questions posed. Guided by teachers, students continually develop their science knowledge. Students should also learn through the inquiry process how to communicate about their own and their peers' investigations and explanations. (Refer to appendix B for an excellent example of ways in which one particularly effective teacher is managing to meaningfully engage students—very at-risk students at that—in science.[3])

There is logic behind the abilities outlined in the inquiry standard, but it requires neither a step-by-step sequence nor scientific method. In practice, student questions might arise from previous investigations, planned classroom activities, or discussions students have with one another. For instance, if children ask one another how animals are similar and different, their discussion may lead to an investigation into characteristics of organisms they can observe.

Full inquiry involves asking a simple question, completing an investigation, answering the question, and presenting the results to others. In the elementary grades, students begin to develop the physical and intellectual abilities of scientific inquiry. They can design investigations to try to see what happens in certain situations—they tend to focus on concrete results of tests and will entertain the idea of a "fair" test (a test in which only one variable at a time is changed). However, children in kindergarten through fourth grade have difficulty with experimentation as a process of testing ideas and the logic of using evidence to formulate explanations.

During their early years, children's natural curiosity leads them to explore the world by observing and manipulating common objects and materials in their environment. Children compare, describe, and sort as they begin to form explanations of the world. Developing a subject-matter knowledge base to explain and predict the world requires many experiences over a long period. Young children bring experiences, understanding, and ideas to school. Teachers then provide opportunities to continue children's explorations in focused settings with other children using simple tools, such as magnifiers and measuring devices.

Developing Student Abilities and Understanding, Grades 5–8

Students in grades 5–8 should have ample opportunities to engage in full and in partial inquiries. In a full inquiry students begin with a question, design an investigation, gather evidence, formulate an answer to the original question, and communicate the investigative process and results. In partial inquiries, they develop abilities and understanding of selected aspects of the inquiry process. For instance, students might describe how they would design an investigation, develop explanations based on scientific information and evidence provided through a classroom activity, or recognize and analyze several alternative explanations for a natural phenomenon presented in a teacher-led demonstration.

At these grade levels, students can begin to recognize the relationship between explanation and evidence. They can understand that background knowledge and theories guide the design of investigations, the types of observations made, and the interpretations of data. In turn, the experiments and investigations become experiences that shape and modify the students' background knowledge.

With an appropriate curriculum and adequate instruction, middle-school students can develop the skills of investigation and the understanding that scientific inquiry is guided by knowledge, observations, ideas, and questions. Middle-school students might have trouble identifying variables and controlling more than one variable in an experiment. Students also might have difficulties understanding the influence of different variables in an experiment—for example, variables that have no effect, marginal effect, or opposite effects on an outcome.

Teachers of science for middle-school students should note that students tend to center on evidence that confirms their current beliefs and concepts (i.e., personal explanations), and ignore or fail to perceive evidence that does not agree with their current concepts. It is important for teachers to challenge current beliefs and concepts and provide scientific explanations as alternatives.

Several factors of this standard should be highlighted. The instructional activities of a scientific inquiry should engage students in identifying and shaping an understanding of the current question. Students should know what the question is asking, what background knowledge is being used to frame the question, and what they will have to do to answer the question. The students' questions should be relevant and meaningful for them. To help focus investigations, students should frame questions such as:

• What do we want to find out about ____?
• How can we make the most accurate observations?
• Is this the best way to answer our questions?
• If we do this, then what do we expect will happen?

The instructional activities of a scientific inquiry should involve students in establishing and refining the methods, materials, and data they will collect. As students conduct investigations and make observations, they should consider questions such as:

- What data will answer the question?
- What are the best observations or measurements to make?

Students should be encouraged to repeat data-collection procedures and to share data among groups.

In middle schools, students produce oral or written reports that present the results of their inquiries. Such reports and discussions should occur frequently in science programs. Students' discussions should center on questions such as:

- How should we organize the data to present the clearest answer to our question?
- How should we organize the evidence to present the strongest explanation?

Out of the discussions about the range of ideas, the background knowledge claims, and the data, the opportunity arises for learners to shape their experiences about the practice of science and the rules of scientific thinking and knowing.

The language and practices evident in the classroom are an important element in conducting inquiries. Students need opportunities to present their abilities and understanding and to use the knowledge and language of science to communicate scientific explanations and ideas. Writing, labeling drawings, completing concept maps, developing spreadsheets, and designing computer graphics should be part of science education. These activities should be presented in a way that allows students to receive constructive feedback on the quality of thought and expression and the accuracy of scientific explanations.

This standard should not be interpreted as advocating a "scientific method." The conceptual and procedural abilities suggest a logical progression, but they do not imply a rigid approach to scientific inquiry. On the contrary, they imply the codevelopment of students' skills in acquiring science knowledge, in using high-level reasoning, in applying existing understanding of scientific ideas, and in communicating scientific information. This standard cannot be met by having the students memorize the abilities and understandings. It can be met only when students frequently engage in active inquiries.

LESSON PLAN STRATEGIES

The next portion of the book provides ideas for developing curriculum that is hands-on, is suitable for small- and large-group work, stimulates girls to ask questions and research answers to their questions, and conforms to district, state, and national science education standards. We may ask what the best strategy is, but as the research demonstrates, there is no one teaching method that is proven to be the "best." Rather, an effective teacher will develop curriculum based on first getting to know his or her students and what their knowledge base is, what the outcomes and standards are, and how he or she will assess the outcomes. The following are just a few of the teaching strategies an effective teacher will employ, and subsequent sections provide descriptions of each, as well as formats, examples, and templates for most.

- Inquiry-based learning
- Problem-based learning
- Direct instruction
- Differentiated instruction
- Constructivism
- Demonstration

These techniques can be used to align with girls' learning styles in particular, but they also should prove successful with boys.

STRATEGIES DEFINED

Inquiry-Based Learning

According to Mary Ann Fitzgerald, an assistant professor in the Department of Instructional Technology at the University of Georgia, and Al Byers, director of the National Science Teachers Association (NSTA) Institute in Arlington, Virginia, "Inquiry is the process scientists use to build an understanding of the natural world. Students can learn about the world using inquiry. Although students rarely discover knowledge that is new to humankind, current research indicates that students engaged in inquiry build knowledge that is new to them. Student inquiry is a multi-facetted activity that involves making observations; posing questions; examining multiple sources of information to see what is already known; planning investigations; reviewing what is already known in light of the student's experimental evidence; using tools to gather, analyze and interpret data; proposing answers, explanations, and predictions; and communicating the results. Inquiry requires identification of assumptions, use of critical and logical thinking, and consideration of alternative explanations."[4]

Note: You will find an inquiry-based lesson plan format later in this chapter along with examples and a template you may follow to develop your own.

Problem-Based Learning

A definition crafted by Virginia Tech University states: "Problem-based learning (PBL) is situated approximately halfway between the social and radical constructivist paradigms. PBL utilizes student groups, but each group member is also responsible for independent research. Further, instructor scaffolding is considerably less direct in problem-based learning than in other constructivist models such as anchored instruction. Students are allowed to struggle and induct their own mental model of course concepts with only occasional 'lifelines' from the instructor when concept processing falls off-track. Problem-based learning is most similar to case-based instruction, but in its purest form, PBL is more open-ended."[5]

Note: You will find a PBL lesson plan format later in this chapter along with a sample and a template you may follow to develop your own.

Direct Instruction

Direct instruction is teacher centered and typically what we think of when we think about a lecture. The teacher talks and the students "listen" (we are never sure if students are listening) and sometimes take notes. There are situations in which direct instruction is appropriate, but the key to effective teaching is to keep the instruction short and to the point, and to move as soon as possible into another strategy that is more hands-on.

Note: You will find a direct instruction lesson plan format later in this chapter along with a template you may follow to develop your own.

Differentiated Instruction

According to Tracey Hall, PhD, senior research scientist with the National Center on Accessing the General Curriculum (NCAC) at the Center for Applied Special Technology (CAST), "To differentiate instruction is to recognize students' varying background knowledge, readiness, language, preferences in learning, interests, and to react responsively. Differentiated instruction is a process to approach teaching and learning for students of differing abilities in the same class. The intent of differentiating instruction is to maximize each student's growth and individual success by meeting each student where he or she is, and assisting in the learning process."[6]

Note: You will find a differentiated instruction lesson plan format—incorporating concept-based learning—later in this chapter along with a template you may follow to develop your own.

Constructivism

This model starts with the student rather than the teacher and asks that the teacher build or construct the learning based on what the student knows. "Constructivism is an approach to teaching, which values developmentally appropriate practices where the learning is child-initiated, child-directed and where the teacher plays a supporting role in the learning."[7]

Note: You will find a little more about this strategy, along with an outline and suggested format you may develop, later in this chapter.

Demonstration

Although putting students in small groups to conduct experiments is always preferable to teacher-led demonstrations, science teachers need to be aware of safety considerations. For example, kindergartners and first graders should not have direct access to fire, so an experiment that shows students what a cloud is by striking a match in a humid environment would be something the teacher or parent volunteers could demonstrate for students.

INQUIRY-BASED LEARNING LESSON PLAN FORMAT

Although today's teachers must incorporate multiple strategies to teach science effectively, particularly to girls, perhaps the strategy that works best in most cases is inquiry-based learning. In their September 2002 *Science Scope* article entitled "A Rubric for Selecting Inquiry-Based Activities," Mary Ann Fitzgerald and Al Byers explain why this is so:

"In the face of today's information explosion, students must acquire the ability to conduct disciplined inquiries based on their own questions. It is no longer possible for educated adults to know everything about a topic, but it is essential that they know how to discover answers to questions that are relevant in their personal and professional lives. Scientific inquiry is one essential tool for discovering answers."[8]

Below is the format of an inquiry-based lesson plan.

1. Targeted Grade or Age Level

Self-Explanatory.

2. Science Topic Addressed

The topic (fact or set of facts, generalization, concept, theory, or law) that will be used as the vehicle for exploring the process identified in item 3.

3. Process-Oriented Objective(s)

A specific objective—or a short list of objectives—written according to the process-oriented skills guidelines developed by the American Association for the Advancement of Science:

* Observing
* Classifying
* Communicating
* Measuring
* Predicting
* Inferring
* Identifying and controlling variables
* Formulating and testing hypotheses
* Interpreting data
* Defining operationally
* Experimenting
* Constructing models

4. What Do I Want Students to Discover?

The scientific fact(s), generalization, concept, or theory students should be able to articulate as a result of the lesson.

5. Description of Introductory Activity and Discussion

Details about how you will introduce the lesson. This should contain details concerning a demonstration or other interest-focusing activity, the initial discussion, directions, and safety and management considerations appropriate for the lesson.

6. Materials Needed

The list of materials is an integral part of the lesson plan; it enables you to assemble all necessary materials each time you conduct the lesson without having to search through the entire lesson plan to determine the necessary materials.

7. Description of Activities

Details of what the students will do to explore the concept and what you will do to help them in their experiences.

8. Typical Discussion Questions

Typical questions you will ask of groups to stimulate their thinking toward the objective.

9. How Students Will Be Encouraged to Investigate on Their Own in the Classroom

What students might do to continue the investigation in greater depth, exploring additional variations, and keeping the explorations going as they investigate the phenomenon fully. These continued explorations can be part of the current lesson, can be held over for the next science class session, or could occur in a science learning center.

10. Expected Conclusions

The goals and objectives you want the students to achieve and the conclusions you expect them to formulate as a result of their investigations.

11. Applications to Real-Life Situations

Answers the question, so what? Often, well-meaning teachers ask students to do activities that have little or no application to their daily lives. If an activity or lesson cannot be applied to students' daily lives, the lesson lacks meaning. Thus, this section of the lesson plan ensures meaningfulness of the lesson to students.

12. Assessment

How will you evaluate students' learning? What evidence will determine what students know and are able to do as a result of this lesson?

SAMPLES OF INQUIRY-BASED LEARNING LESSON PLANS

The following inquiry-based lesson plans were developed by preservice elementary- and middle-school student teachers at the College of St. Catherine for an in-class microteaching experience. The plans presented here are the revisions that followed delivery and peer evaluation. KWL, which is mentioned in some of these lesson plans, is an active-learning strategy that can be used to guide instruction and also be used as an assessment at the end of a lesson or unit:

- K: What do I *know*?
- W: What do I *want* to know?
- L: What have I *learned*?

Inquiry-Based Lesson Plan #1

Permission to reproduce this lesson plan was granted by Jenna Madden.

1. Targeted Grade and Age Level: Grade 2, Ages 8–9

2. Science Topic Addressed: The Water Cycle

3. Process-Oriented Objectives

Constructing models: Students will be able to construct a miniature water cycle model by following instructions given by the teacher.

   Observing: Students will observe what is happening with their water cycle model and record observations on a worksheet.

   Classifying: Students will start to classify the different forms of water (solid, liquid, gas) and classify water changes by labeling them with the steps of the water cycle.

Predicting: Students will make their own predictions about what changes will occur within their miniature water cycle models.

Experimenting: Students will discuss and hypothesize what will happen when one water cycle model is placed in the sun and another model is placed in the shade. If time permits, they will do the experiment that day. If not, the experiment will be completed in science class the next day.

Measuring: The students will measure an amount of water (in millileters) to put into their large containers.

4. What Do I Want Students to Discover?

The students will learn what a cycle is and connect that to the process of the water cycle. The students will become familiar with the terms: cycle, evaporation, vapor, condensation, precipitation, transpiration, and groundwater. Through reading and using a visual aid of the water cycle, students will develop knowledge about the steps of the water cycle and start to become familiar with putting those steps in order. After creating a model of the water cycle, students will discover what happens as water changes forms and goes through the steps of the cycle.

5. Description of Introductory Activity and Discussion

The teacher will introduce the lesson by telling the class that today they will be learning about the water cycle. The teacher will ask the class if anyone knows anything about the water cycle and record it on the KWL sheet. Then, she will ask the class what they would like to know about the water cycle and she will record that on the KWL sheet as well. The teacher will mention that at the end of the lesson, she will record what the class learned on the KWL sheet. Next, the teacher will read the book to the class (leaving the last page until the end of the lesson). The teacher will ask the students questions about the story and students will engage in discussion about what happened to the snowflake in the story. Then, the teacher will also explain vocabulary to the class as a way to introduce the topic of the water cycle.

6. Materials Needed

- Piece of large paper to use as a KWL sheet (instead of using a piece of paper, the teacher could write on the blackboard)
- The book *The Snowflake: A Water Cycle Story* by Neil Waldman
- One diagram of the water cycle for the teacher to display (large enough for the class to see)
- One clean baby food jar per student
- One clear bowl per student
- Piece of plastic wrap per student (to fit over the top opening of a clear bowl)
- One small weight per student
- Water
- One rubber band per student
- One observation sheet per student
- Materials for teacher's miniature water cycle (bowl, jar, rubber band, weight, plastic wrap)
- Set of strips of paper with one step of the water cycle on each (one set per group)
- Masking tape and black markers (a few for the class to share)

7. Description of Activities

1. After the teacher reads the book to the class and discusses vocabulary, she will show the class a simple diagram that outlines an example of the water cycle, and discuss how the steps of the water cycle related

to the story. The teacher will explain how the water cycle is a way in which the earth recycles its water and will relate that concept to how people recycle products. The class will also discuss the importance of water conservation and how students can conserve water at home and at school.

2. Next, the class will follow the teacher's instructions to construct a miniature water cycle model. The students will make predictions of what will happen within the model, draw a picture of their model, and record observations. Then they will place their models on a sunny area of the windowsill in the classroom or outside in the sun.

3. The teacher will divide students into groups of four and give each group strips of paper containing sentences about the steps of the water cycle on them. She will ask the groups to work together to put the sentences in order. She will assist the students and answer any questions they have.

4. The students will observe their water cycle models twice more if time permits; otherwise, they will do so later in the day or the next day in science class or during free time. The students draw a picture of their model and record observations and changes each time.

5. The class and teacher will discuss what has taken place inside their models and the students will share any similarities or differences their models had compared to others'.

6. The teacher will read the last page of the book and quickly review vocabulary by asking students to define the terms they talked about in the lesson. She will then ask the students what they learned that day about the water cycle, and record their answers on the KWL sheet as closure to the lesson.

8. Typical Discussion Questions

- What happened to the snowflake in the story? What are some ways in which we can conserve water? At home? In the classroom? At school in general?
- What do people do to recycle and reuse products? Why do we recycle?
- What is a cycle?
- What do you think will happen to your miniature water cycle model? What changes will occur? Make your own prediction and record it on your observation sheet.
- Do you think evaporation will occur? If so, how long do you think it will take for the water to evaporate? If you don't think the water will evaporate, explain your reasoning.
- Do you think the changes within the water cycle model would be different if the air were warmer or cooler than it is today?
- What changes, if any, have you observed within your water cycle model?
- Can anyone give me a real-life example of condensation that you have seen?
- Think about how direct sunlight affects evaporation.
- Does it matter if the water cycle model was placed in the sun or in the shade?
- Would water in a model in the sun take longer to evaporate than a model in the shade, or vice versa?

9. How Students Will Be Encouraged to Investigate on Their Own in the Classroom

- Students will make their own predictions as to what will occur within their water cycle models.
- Students will observe their models and record their observations individually.
- Students will be encouraged to look at their models from different perspectives and jot down any questions they have related to the water cycle.
- During free time, students will get a chance to investigate the water cycle a bit more by utilizing the water cycle station (a table set up with models and information on the water cycle for students to look at and study). Also during free time, students will be allowed to do research on the water cycle by exploring the

website and looking at different books on the water cycle. This would be a fun way to spend free time and for the students to find other projects and experiments about the water cycle that they could do in the classroom or at home.

10. Expected Conclusions

Using the book, discussion, diagram, and observation of their own models, the students will learn how the water cycle functions. After observing their models a few times, the students will see that the water from the bowl evaporates and condenses onto the plastic and then "precipitates" into the smaller container. Some models may not work as well as others due to construction mistakes and placement on the windowsills (some models may get more sunlight than others).

11. Applications to Real-Life Situations

The teacher can explain the connection between the water cycle and pollution, and discuss the impact that polluted water has on the environment and the water cycle. The class can also discuss the importance of water conservation and how water is a resource that is necessary for life. The teacher can encourage students to conserve water in their daily routines, such as by turning off the faucet while brushing their teeth and turning off the water while they are shampooing their hair in the shower.

12. Assessment

1. The students in each group will try to put in order the steps of the water cycle after the steps have been explained by the teacher and discussed. The teacher will walk around the classroom to see if the students understand the activity and the steps. The teacher will offer assistance to those students who may be having trouble, and won't expect the students to put all the steps in order right away because this is just the first lesson on the topic.

2. The teacher will watch as the students construct their models and observe the changes. The teacher will also look at the observation sheets to make sure that students have recorded their predictions and observations and drawn diagrams of their model. She will also check for spelling and grammar mistakes.

3. At the end of the lesson, the teacher will ask the students to define vocabulary words they learned in the lesson as a review (such as *condensation, groundwater, precipitation*). The teacher will read the last page of the book as a conclusion to the lesson. Finally, asking students to comment on things they learned about the water cycle, she will record those items on the L section of the KWL sheet.

Resources

The Snowflake: A Water Cycle Story by Neil Waldman (ISBN: 0761323473)

www.proteacher.com/dragonfly/water/watercycle.html (This website shows how to make the miniature water cycle model and includes facts about the water cycle.)

www.coreknowledge.org/CK/resrcs/lessons/2.htm (This website is from the 2003 Core Knowledge National Conference, "Take a Spin around the Water Cycle, Grade 2." It contains ideas for different lesson plans and water cycle units.)

Inquiry-Based Lesson Plan #2

Permission to reprint this lesson plan was granted by Bridgette Healy.

1. Targeted Grade Level: Grade 5

2. Science Topic Addressed: Density Rainbow

3. Process-Oriented Objectives

- Construct a density rainbow by layering colored fluids that rest on one another because of differing density.
- Experiment by dropping different objects and materials into their density rainbows.
- Make predictions about where the different objects will land.
- Observe the layers that each object lands in.
- Draw a diagram to show what students observe.
- Make inferences about the densities of different materials and liquids.
- Determine that different objects have different densities in relation to the fluids.
- Communicate ideas about density through active participation in class discussion and by answering questions on a handout.

4. What Do I Want Students to Discover?

- Different materials and fluids have different densities.
- An object that is less dense than a liquid will float.
- An object that is denser than a liquid will sink.
- Students will gain a greater understanding of the concept of density.

5. Description of Introductory Activity and Discussion

- Read a story about Archimedes and density from the book *Science Lab in a Supermarket* by Bob Friedhoffer.
- Define density: "Density is a measure of how much material of an object is packed into a given volume, calculated by dividing the mass of an object by its volume."
- Explain floating and sinking: "Tap water has a density of 1.0 g/cm^3. Any object with a density less than 1.0 g/cm^3 will float. An object with a density greater than 1.0 g/cm^3 will sink."
- Demonstration: Students will observe as I fill two identical glasses, one with isopropyl alcohol and one with tap water. Next, I will ask students to predict what will happen when I drop a piece of candle wax into the water. I will drop the wax into the water and students will observe that it floats. Then, I will ask students to predict what will happen when I drop the wax into the alcohol. I will drop it in and students will observe that the wax sinks in the alcohol.
- Discussion: The class will discuss reasons why the candle wax floats in water but sinks in alcohol and make inferences about the density of the isopropyl alcohol and the candle wax in relation to the water (tap water 1.0 g/cm^3, candle wax 0.85 g/cm^3, isopropyl alcohol 0.76 g/cm^3).
- Students will be asked to think of any questions they have or things they want to know related to density and write them in their notebooks.
- Students will divide up into small groups for the density rainbow activity.

6. Materials Needed

- Instruction handout
- Prediction handout
- Observation handout
- Discussion Question Handout
- *Science in a Supermarket* by Bob Friedhoffer
- Introductory demonstration materials: two glasses, isopropyl alcohol, tap water, two pieces of candle wax
- Density rainbow materials: tall glass, measuring cup, spoon, food coloring (three colors), corn syrup, glycerin, tap water, vegetable oil, a variety of small objects to experiment with (eraser pieces, candle wax, M&Ms, thumbtacks, sunflower seeds, Reese's Pieces, beads, foam, paper clips, noodles, minute rice, pencil lead, pennies)

7. Description of Activities

Students will construct a density rainbow by following instructions (see handout). I will facilitate by reading though the instructions step-by-step as the class performs them. Once students have completed their models I will ask them to look at the different objects I have given them, and predict where each will land when dropped into the density rainbow. Students will record their predictions by making a diagram on the prediction handout provided. Once they have completed their predictions students will be free to experiment on their own by dropping different materials into the liquid. Students will make observations and diagram them. During this time, I will ask questions to get students thinking about the properties of density and can be inferred from observation. Afterward, I will have students answer questions on a handout, then lead a class discussion during which students will communicate their answers and what they have learned about density. The class will discuss the differences in their predictions and what they observed. I will also ask students to refer to their notebooks and to discuss any unanswered questions. The class will also discuss questions that were answered through the experimentation process and how. I will follow up with some questions to get students thinking about density in some real-life situations.

8. Typical Discussion Questions

- If the liquids were poured in a different order, would the layers end up the same?
- Can two objects be exactly the same size but have different densities?
- Why do some things sink and others float?
- Which objects and fluids have a density greater than 1.0 g/cm³?
- Which objects and fluids have a density less than 1.0 g/cm³?
- Were the results of your experimenting as you expected? What predictions were you right and wrong about?
- What is happening with the minute rice? Can you explain why this is happening?
- Which objects are denser than corn syrup?
- Which objects are less dense than corn oil?
- Are the densities of Reese's Pieces and M&Ms similar? How do they compare to the density of the fluids?

9. How Students Will Be Encouraged to Investigate on Their Own in the Classroom

I will provide additional activities that allow students to further investigate and experiment with density during other class periods.

Additional activity 1: Place one diet soda and one regular soda in a sink full of water. Observe the results and discuss.

Additional activity 2: Place an egg in a glass of tap water. It will sink. Slowly add several spoonfuls of salt to the water. Observe the results and discuss.

10. Expected Conclusions

- Students will determine that different objects have different densities in relation to the fluids.
- Students will understand that an object will float in a liquid if it is denser than the liquid and sink if it is less dense.
- Students draw inferences about which objects and liquids have similar densities.
- Students will gain an understanding of the concept of density and some of its properties.

11. Applications to Real-Life Situations

I will ask the following questions to facilitate a class discussion about density in the following real-life situations:

- What do you know about the density of the human body? How does it relate to the density of water?
- People say they are more buoyant in the ocean than in other water. Have you ever experienced this? What might explain this?
- Why is it easier to do a handstand in a swimming pool than on dry land?
- Why does a helium-filled balloon rise in the air, while a balloon filled with air from your mouth sinks to the floor?
- Can you think of any other situations that can be explained by differing densities?

12. Assessment

- Students will make a diagram to show their observations.
- Students will answer questions on a worksheet.
- Students will communicate their ideas though class discussion.

Handout #1: Density Rainbow Instructions

You will be layering colored fluids that rest on one another because of differing density. The secret to this project is to pour the fluids carefully enough not to disturb the previous layer. You will begin with the heaviest fluid of the group, corn syrup, and end with the lightest fluid, vegetable oil. Follow these steps carefully to create your own density rainbow:

1. Corn syrup layer

   - Pour an inch or two of corn syrup into a measuring cup.
   - Add a few drops of food coloring and stir.
   - Pour it into the glass.
   - Rinse the measuring cup.

2. Glycerin layer

   - Pour an inch or two of glycerin into the measuring cup.
   - Add a few drops of another color of food coloring and stir.

- Use the spoon to place the glycerin on top of the syrup by holding the spoon in the glass (without touching the syrup) and pouring the glycerin gently onto the spoon. This helps to diffuse the liquid more gently than pouring the glycerin directly onto the syrup.
- Rinse the measuring cup.

3. Water layer

- Pour an inch or two of tap water into the measuring cup.
- Add a few drops of another color of food coloring and stir.
- Place the water onto the glycerin layer with the spoon as before.

4. Vegetable Oil Layer

- Food coloring will not mix with oil, so leave it natural.
- Using the spoon, add an inch or two of the vegetable oil to the glass.

You should now have four bright layers of different fluids! Before you move on with your experiment, make sure you complete the prediction handout. After completing the prediction handout, move on to the observation handout.

Handout #2: Prediction Handout

Look at the various small objects you have been given. Before you do any experimenting, try to predict where each of the objects will land in the density rainbow. Make a diagram to show your predictions.

Handout #3: Observation Handout

Here's the fun part: Drop the different items into the glass and watch which layers they land in. Make a diagram to show what you observe.

Discussion Questions

- If the liquids were poured in a different order, would the layers end up the same?
- Can two objects be exactly the same size but have different densities?
- Why do some things sink and others float?
- Which objects and fluids have a density greater than 1.0 g/cm^3?
- Which objects and fluids have a density less than 1.0 g/cm^3?
- Were the results of your experimenting as you expected? What predictions were you right and wrong about?
- What is happening with the minute rice? Can you explain why this is happening?
- Which objects are denser than corn syrup?
- Which objects are less dense than corn oil?
- Are the densities of Reese's Pieces and M&Ms similar? How do they compare to the density of the fluids?

Inquiry-Based Lesson Plan #3

Permission to reprint this lesson plan was granted by Kristin Sieg.

1. Targeted Grade or Age Level: Grades 3–4

2. Science Topic Addressed: Exploring Magnets and Magnetism

- Magnets are pieces of metal that have the power to attract other pieces of metal.
- Magnets attract objects made of iron or steel (which is made of iron).
- Magnets contain two opposite poles (north and south).
- Like poles push away, or repel.
- Opposite poles pull together, or attract.

3. Process-Oriented Objectives

- Students will observe the properties of magnets.
- Students will understand that objects can be sorted and classified based on their properties.
- Students will identify and classify objects attracted and not attracted by magnets.
- Students will predict objects that will be attracted and not attracted by magnets.
- Student will observe that push and pull forces can make objects move.

4. What Do I Want Students to Discover?

- Magnets are pieces of metal that have the power to attract other pieces of metal.
- Without touching them, a magnet pulls on all things made of iron and either pushes or pulls on other magnets.
- Magnets attract and repel one another and certain kinds of other materials.

5. Description of Introductory Activity and Discussion

- List objects that magnets can pull.
- Discussion questions: Have you ever played with a magnet? If so, what were you able to do with it? What do you know about magnets? How can you find out which objects magnets can pull?
- Show the students a variety of magnets.
- Discuss various magnets and their common uses.

  ° Kitchens: automatic can openers have magnets to hold opened can lids.
  ° Cabinet doors stay closed because of magnets.
  ° Some people wear magnetic earrings.
  ° Many toys contain magnets.
  ° At school, speakers, magnetic paper holders, and some games also have magnets.
  ° Many electronic devices contain magnetic material (VHS and cassette tapes, computers, cell phones, electrical motors and generators).

- Introduce vocabulary terms throughout the discussion: a *magnet* is a stone or piece of metal that attracts some other metal (there are both natural and man-made magnets); to *attract* means to pull toward; to *repel* means to push away.
- Before passing out materials, discuss safety issues (i.e., using caution with nails and other sharp objects).

6. *Materials Needed*

- Various types and sizes of magnets
- Magnetic and nonmagnetic objects and materials for testing (steel nails, aluminum nails, straws, cardboard, coins, rubber bands, plastic spoons, silver spoons, assorted paper clips, etc.)

7. *Description of Activities*

- First, divide students into groups of two to four, depending on the amount of materials available. Next, instruct students on how to complete the exploration activity and corresponding worksheet, shown in figure 4.1. The directions for student exploration follow.

  1. Take out the objects from only one bag now.
  2. Touch your magnet to each object. Observe whether or not the object is attracted to the magnet.
  3. Complete the worksheet for each object in the first bag. Record the name of the object, the material of the object, and whether the object is attracted to the magnet or not.
  4. Discussion questions:

     ° Which objects are pulled by the magnet?
     ° Which objects are not pulled by the magnet?
     ° How are the objects in the pulled group alike?
     ° Can you make a rule about which objects your magnet pulls?

  5. Conclusions:

     ° Magnets are pieces of metal that have the power to attract other pieces of metal (iron or steel).
     ° Common metals that are not attracted by magnets are brass, aluminum, tin, silver, stainless steel, copper, bronze, and gold.

  6. Explain that magnets have two opposite (north and south) poles (ends). (They have positive and negative charges.)
  7. Put the objects back into the bag. Put the bag away.
  8. Take out the objects from the second bag.
  9. Discussion questions:

     ° Which do you think your magnet will pull?
     ° Which will it not pull?

  10. On your worksheet, predict whether or not the objects in the second bag will be attracted to the magnet.
  11. Now use your magnet on the objects in each group.
  12. Discussion question: Was every object in the correct group?
  13. Make any needed corrections to your worksheet.
  14. Review the vocabulary terms and the properties of magnets.
  15. Instruct students to complete their worksheets by writing two sentences telling what they found out about magnets. (Students who finish early can write about what was interesting to them.)

8. *Typical Discussion Questions*

- What do you know about magnets?
- Which objects are pulled by the magnet?

Name: _____   Date: _____

Name of Object	Material of Object	Attraction to Magnet			
		Prediction		Observation	
		Yes	No	Yes	No

Write two sentences telling what you found out about magnets.

1.
2.

Figure 4.1.   Magnets Worksheet

- Which objects are not pulled by the magnets
- What do the objects that magnets pull have in common?
- How are magnets used at school? In your home?
- Are magnets important? Why or why not?

9. How Students Will Be Encouraged to Investigate on Their Own in the Classroom

- Students will be encouraged to discover other objects around the classroom that their magnet will pull. Students will also be encouraged to find magnets in their home and to explore different objects that are attracted to and repelled by magnets.
- In following unit lessons, students will learn about magnetic separations, the power of magnets, and how to make magnets.
- Students will be informed of resources where they may find additional information on magnets (i.e., websites and books).

10. Expected Conclusions

- Students will understand the basic properties of magnets.
- Students will be able to identify objects that will be attracted to and repelled by magnets.

11. Applications to Real-Life Situations

- Magnetism is an essential building block of physics.
- The principles of magnetism are contained in many present-day devices that contain motors, electrical energy production and transmission, computers, or computer disks.
- Magnets are also present in simpler technologies such as the compass.

12. Assessment

- Students will complete and turn in their worksheets.
- Students will complete a journal entry about magnets at school and in their homes.

Inquiry-Based Lesson Plan #4

Permission to reprint this lesson plan was granted by Janelle Jacques.

1. Grade Level: First Grade

2. Science Topic Addressed: What Can Be Learned from an Egg?

3. Process-Oriented Objectives

Students make observations about eggs through taking measurements, following directions, making observations, and then making a conclusion.

4. What Do I Want Students to Discover?

Students will first start by telling what they already "know." The class will use measuring, observations, and inferences to discover ways to learn more about the object.

5. Description of Introductory Activity and Discussion

I will begin with the KWL exercise asking such questions as:

- What do you think you know about an egg?
- Are all eggs the same size?

I will record the responses in the K column. I will tell the students how they can learn much more about an object by using scientific experiments like measurements and simply using their eyes to observe. I will explain what "observations" are, so that everyone is clear. I will advise the students to be careful with their eggs and not to break them—but promise they will get to break one at some point during the experiment. I will also fill in the W portion of the KWL so I can learn what they would like to know.

6. Materials Needed

- Three eggs per student (two hard boiled for measuring and rolling, one for breaking)
- Three six-inch pieces of yarn
- Newspaper
- Three low, wide-mouthed jars
- Three rulers
- Warm water
- Three permanent markers
- Three aluminum containers
- Handout for each student
- Whiteboard for KWL

7. Description of Activities

First, all the students will pick out their eggs (three per student). I will ask them to observe their egg and say whether or not their eggs all look alike. Can they say anything about their eggs that are different? I will instruct students to use their yarn to measure the width and the length of their eggs. I will explain what "width" and "length" mean. I will demonstrate how to measure and instruct them to use their markers to mark their yarn to record their measurements in inches and then to compare the marked yarn to the ruler and transfer that information onto their handout.

I can allow students to "partner up" for the measuring activity because measuring a round egg is a difficult task. Each student will record the findings on a worksheet. Once the students have completed recording their measurements, I will ask them to read all three of their measurements aloud.

Second, each student will take a sheet of newspaper and find a spot on the floor with plenty of room between and around him or her. I will again caution them to be gentle with their eggs. I will tell them to observe how their eggs move when they roll them along the floor on the newspaper. After I allow them about one or two minutes to observe their eggs rolling, I will ask them to describe how they roll and move. I will record their answers on another poster board.

Third, the class will scrutinize an eggshell. I will ask students to remark, aloud, descriptions of their egg(s). After the students describe the shells, I will ask them if anyone's eggshell has holes in it.

The next experiment will be instructing the students to fill their low, wide-mouthed jars halfway with warm water. Prior to telling the students to put an egg in the jar, I will ask them what they think will happen to the egg when it is submerged in the water bath. They will carry the jars back to their desk and gently place one of their eggs in their jar. I will instruct them to look closely at the egg and say what they see. Once they begin to see bubbles I will ask the students to take note of whether their egg is floating or sinking.

I will now distribute the aluminum pans and tell the students the time has come for them to finally break their eggs. I will demonstrate how to crack an egg. I will instruct the students to crack one of their eggs into the pans and look closely at what they see. I want them to notice the parts, textures, and colors of the egg. The students must also look closely at the inside of the shell.

For closure, the class will have a discussion (described below). The class will then clean up by putting the unused eggs back into the carton and disposing of the cracked ones and the string. They will empty the water from the jars and put them away, and do the same with the rulers, rinsed-out tins, and markers. Students will turn in to the teacher their measurements so she can use them to assess student progress.

8. Typical Discussion Questions

From the first experiment, I will ask such questions as: After measuring your eggs and hearing everyone's answers, are all eggs the same? Tell me again the difference between length and width.

For the second part, I will ask: Why do the eggs wobble, how far did they get, did any go in circles, and why is it important that the eggs not fall from the trees? I will tell them how the function of the egg's shape is to keep the eggs close to their mothers in their nest.

For the third section, I will ask the students to observe the bubbles and tell me why bubbles are forming. I will ask them where the bubbles are forming and ask them what they think it means. I will also want them to notice which side (if any) of their egg is upright. Is it floating? Why do you think it is or is not? What does that mean about what is on the inside of it?

For the last part, the cracking of the egg, I will ask the students where the air sac is, where the yolk is, and where the egg white is. I will make sure the students can notice all of the parts. I will ask them to describe the feeling of both the egg and the inside of the shell and instruct them to note the air sac. I will ask why it is important for eggs to have an air sac. The class will then discuss why air sacs are important to baby birds that may live inside eggs, and how the holes are how the birds get oxygen. I will conclude the discussion with the final L portion of the KWL poster, discuss any findings, answer any additional questions, and finally, collect the worksheets.

9. How Students Will Be Encouraged to Investigate on Their Own in the Classroom

Students could explore what happens to an egg by doing various things to it. For example, they could poke a hole in it with a pin and see what happens to the inside, or they could cook it in various ways, like poaching or scrambling, and see how it changes in appearance. They could even try this experiment at home with other objects, like apples, lemons, or even balls, to see if the objects are uniform.

10. Expected Conclusions

The students should gain an understanding that objects aren't always what they appear to be. They may all look alike from the outside, but when investigated further, they are all unique. Students should gain an understanding of observing, measuring, touching, and manipulating objects to gain a better understanding of them. The class will conclude that all eggs are a little different and that using scientific experiments is a good way to make these kinds of discoveries.

11. Applications to Real-Life Situations

Students should be able to connect the main principle to people, in that everybody is unique, even if their height, skin color, or hair color is similar. It is hoped that students can learn that it is interesting to look closely at everyday items and that there is a lot to be learned from such items. It is desired that students learn to be critical of objects and curious about them. Students should be able to measure and learn ways to measure all shapes by using, for example, an easy yarn-and-ruler method as was used in this experiment.

12. Assessment

Most assessments will be based on the participation of the group. I will fill in the students' responses to the K category and determine if they understand. I will use the worksheet to ensure the students learned measuring correctly.

PROBLEM-BASED LEARNING LESSON PLAN FORMAT

PBL requires students—working in groups—to solve authentic, open-ended problems with many potential solutions. It emphasizes students' preexisting knowledge ("start with what you know") and requires them to actively participate by helping plan, organize, and evaluate the problem-solving process. Rather than relying on a structured set of requisite resources, students need access to many resources for research. In fact, deciding on what they need to know to solve a problem and pursuing research strategies are important elements of the PBL process. The informational gaps that students identify become learning issues that the group divides up for further research. By nature, PBL has an interdisciplinary flavor, typically pulling in information from various subject domains. This leads to above-average retention, excellent integration of knowledge, and above all, development of lifelong learning skills such as how to evaluate multiple options, how to research, how to communicate in groups, and how to handle problems.

You will find a gold mine of outstanding resources on problem-based learning at the URL education.nmsu .edu/projects/hrsa/pages/pbl.htm. This site leads to more than seventy resources, including several dozen websites, almost as many journal articles (several of which are accessible online), and a handful of books.

This PBL lesson plan format and the sample that follows came from www.aug.edu/teacher_development/ PBL/Elementary%20Units/Courtyard/Plants.htm,[9] an Augusta State University website that is no longer active.

- Subject(s)
- Grade Level
- Theme
- Quality Core Curriculum (QCC) Objective(s)
- Lesson Objective(s)
- Learner Outcomes (life performance skills)
- Assessment (reflecting objectives and outcomes)
- Introduction (assessing and building on prior knowledge; motivating students)
- Procedures (how to engage students in the learning process to meet diverse student needs)
- Closure (involving students in reflection, metacognition, and goal setting)
- Materials and Resources

Sample of Problem-Based Learning Lesson Plan
- Subject(s): Science
- Grade Level: Grade 4
- Theme: Plants

- QCC Objective(s): Explain the process of photosynthesis and its importance to plants and animals, and define relationships in living communities and how changes occur.
- Lesson Objective(s): Students will identify what a bulb is and how to plant one.
- Learner Outcomes (life performance skills): Students will learn to work as a team to research a question and develop solutions.
- Assessment (reflecting objectives and outcomes): A letter will be written to Mrs. Hill explaining what bulbs we should plant in our courtyard.
- Introduction (assessing and building on prior knowledge; motivating students): Mrs. Hill's letter was read to the students; then they developed a web of the information needed to solve the problem.
- Procedures (how to engage students in the learning process to meet diverse student needs.): The students were divided into groups of four, meeting needs of all level abilities. Each group searched the web for answers and looked in encyclopedias and other gardening books.
- Closure (involving students in reflection, metacognition, and goal setting): Letters were developed and a self-evaluation rubric was used.
- Materials and Resources: The web, reference books, and gardening books were used.

DIRECT INSTRUCTION LESSON PLAN FORMAT

The following lesson plan format for direct instruction was drawn from a Seton Hall University website: education.shu.edu/pt3grant/zinicola/lessonplanformat.html.[10]

1. Title of Lesson

This can be in the form of a question.

2. Overall Goals

For example:

- To give children the scope, sizes and distances of planets in the solar system
- To present activities whereby students discover that matter can be classified by states
- To reinforce the idea of a complete circuit through trial and error
- To demonstrate the formation of a cloud in a jar as an example of evaporation and condensation
- To use models for students to discover why we experience seasonal change
- To use prisms to determine the colors of the spectrum in white light

3. Learning Objectives

Include specific process skills to indicate what the students will be able to do or demonstrate as a result of this lesson, for example:

- Measure the scale distance of the planets in inches
- Contrast the sizes of the nine planets and make generalizations
- Classify rocks according to specific properties

- Use models to enact rotation and revolution
- Communicate through writing and speaking the steps of the water cycle
- Fold a paper airplane to make it go straight up and straight down with a horizontal thrust
- Measure the temperature of the room in degrees Celsius and Fahrenheit
- Compare the lengths of two plants

4. Purpose and Rationale

Ask yourself:

- Why am I teaching this lesson this way?
- What are the significance, relevance, and reason for teaching and learning this lesson?
- What are the standards that are addressed in this lesson?

5. Teacher Preparation

Describes what you must do (such as research, purchasing, and organization) to get ready for this lesson.

6. Materials and Resources

Develop a list that includes quantities and resources of:

- Supplies
- Handouts
- Lab sheets
- Videotapes or audiotapes
- Software programs
- Internet sites
- Books
- Magazines or journals
- Encyclopedias

7. Procedure

Step 1: Introduction:

- Make connections between prior knowledge and experiences with what is presented.
- Find out what students' ideas are on this topic; expose misconceptions.
- Review what was learned in prior lessons and then introduce content and vocabulary necessary for *this* lesson.
- Use teaching charts, video clips, books, presentation software, instructional software, articles, tapes, overhead projector, handouts, models, and so on to accent instruction.
- Create and describe the structure for group learning (if applicable), whole-class discussion, and individual work (journal, worksheet).

Step 2: Exploration:

- Describe in detail the activity or investigation students will pursue, giving them clear directions.
- Describe the path of inquiry or process of discovery to be followed.
- List the questions you will ask.
- Prepare a lab sheet for students to record data and answer questions.
- Have students (a) predict and explain, (b) explore and discuss, and then (c) revise their explanations and theories.
- Conclude, share results, discuss, ask and answer questions, evaluate lesson, and assess student understanding.

Step 3: Application:

- How can the student apply to personal experience what was learned today?
- How can the value of this lesson be made relevant in the students' lives?
- What are good follow-up activities to reinforce concepts learned?

Part of the application step is assessment:

- How do you know if your students learned? Design a worksheet, journal recording, test, quiz, or performance-based activity for students to demonstrate what they have learned.
- Have your overall goals and learning objectives been met?
- What alternative activities will you use for students who need additional help?
- How do you intend to extend the lesson: dig deeper, go beyond—with relevant homework, classwork, parent-involvement activity, research assignment, and so on?

Another part of the application step is self-evaluation:

- Reflect on strengths and weaknesses of the lesson as taught.
- Describe individual student responses to techniques used. How did they react?
- Discuss student "thinking" and ideas.
- Include samples of students' answers on lab sheet or journal entry (photocopy is fine).
- Ask students for a brief evaluation of lesson. Include their responses.
- Discuss fulfilled and unfulfilled expectations. Were there any surprises?
- Having already reflected on the lesson, how would you modify it?

DIFFERENTIATED (CONCEPT-BASED) LESSON PLAN FORMAT

Before using the following format, a teacher might find it helpful to conduct some research about the differentiated process. Recommended are: *The Differentiated Classroom: Responding to the Needs of All Learners* by Carol Ann Tomlinson (Association for Supervision & Curriculum Development, 1999. ISBN: 0871203421), and *Differentiating Instruction in the Regular Classroom: How to Reach and Teach All Learners Grades 3–12* by Diane Heacox (Free Spirit, 2002. ISBN: 1575421186). The following lesson plan format—which incorporates differentiated instruction into a concept-based learning theory—came from a site sponsored by Randolph-Macon College: faculty.rmwc.edu/mentor_grant/Differentiated/lesson_template.htm.[11]

- Title
- Developed by
- Grade Level
- Key Concept
- Planning—what students will know (standards and content), understand (principles and generalizations), and be able to do (objectives and outcomes)
- Essential Questions
- Instruction: How the planning is implemented
- Preassessment Strategies
- Anticipatory Set
- Differentiated Learning Experiences
- Assessment and Culminating Performance
- Closure
- Resources
- Approximate Time Span

CONSTRUCTIVIST INQUIRY-BASED SCIENCE LESSON PLAN FORMAT

Rather than assuming students need some sort of teaching in order to move toward practice and mastery, lesson plans of this type assume that well-crafted lessons engage student interest and activate prior knowledge right away, thus allowing immediate exploration. Here is a general outline of the instructional procedures of such lesson plans:

1. Introduction Phase
2. Puzzling Situation
3. Data Gathering and Experimentation by Students
4. Hypothesizing and Explaining
5. Analyzing the Inquiry Process

Note: The above was drawn from a San Diego State University (SDSU) website, (edweb.sdsu.edu/Courses/EDTEC470/sections/F02-10/lesson_planning.htm),[12] which was last updated in 2002. Jim Julius, who maintains the site, has taught educational technology courses to preservice and in-service teachers and administrators at SDSU and at the University of San Diego. In August 2005, he was named SDSU's associate director of Instructional Technology Services. He was formerly a technical consultant at the USD School of Leadership and Education Sciences and coordinator of USD's Center for Learning and Teaching. At the time of his appointment, Julius was working toward his doctorate in educational technology through the joint SDSU-USD EdD program.

SCIENCE LESSON PLAN TEMPLATES

Below you will find a variety of lesson plan templates that incorporate best practices for how girls learn. Each lesson plan strategy appears as a template or form that you may photocopy for your own use.

INQUIRY-BASED LEARNING SCIENCE LESSON PLAN TEMPLATE

Targeted Grade or Age Level: _____

Science Topic Addressed: _____

Process-Oriented Objective(s): _____

_____

_____

What Do I Want Students to Discover? _____

_____

Description of Introductory Activity and Discussion: _____

_____

_____

_____

Materials Needed: _____ _____

_____ _____

_____ _____

_____ _____

_____ _____

Description of Activities: _____

_____

_____

_____

_____

_____

_____

Typical Discussion Questions: _____

_____

_____

_____

How Students Will Be Encouraged to
Investigate on Their Own in the Classroom: _____

_____

_____

_____

Expected Conclusions: _____

_____

_____

_____

Applications to Real-Life Situations: _____

_____

_____

_____

Assessment: _____

_____

_____

_____

PROBLEM-BASED LEARNING SCIENCE LESSON PLAN TEMPLATE

Subject(s): _____

Grade Level: _____

Theme: _____

Quality Core Curriculum Objective(s): _____

_____

Lesson Objective(s): _____

_____

Learner Outcomes (life performance skills): _____

_____

Assessment: _____

_____

Introduction: _____

_____

Procedures: _____

_____

Closure: _____

_____

Materials Needed: _____ _____

_____ _____

_____ _____

DIRECT INSTRUCTION SCIENCE LESSON PLAN TEMPLATE

The following template was drawn from a Seton Hall University website, education.shu.edu/pt3grant/zinicola/
lessonplanformat.html.

Title of Lesson: _____

Overall Goals: _____
_____
_____
_____

Theme: _____

Learning Objectives: _____
_____
_____

Purpose and Rationale: _____
_____
_____

Teacher Preparation: _____
_____
_____

Materials Needed: _____   _____
_____   _____
_____   _____
_____   _____
_____   _____

Procedure Step 1: Introduction: _____
_____
_____

Procedure Step 2: Exploration: _____
_____
_____

Procedure Step 3: Application: _____
_____
_____

Assessment: _____
_____
_____

Self-Evaluation: _____
_____
_____

DIFFERENTIATED (CONCEPT-BASED) LESSON PLAN TEMPLATE

This template comes from Tracey Hall, PhD, senior research scientist at NCAC, and can be found at www.cast
.org/publications/ncac/ncac_diffinstruc.html.

Title: _____

Developed By: _____

Grade Level: _____

Key Concept: _____

_____

_____

_____

Planning: What students will know: _____

_____

_____

Planning: What students will understand: _____

_____

_____

Essential Questions: _____

_____

_____

Instruction: _____

_____

_____

Preassessment Strategies: _____

_____

_____

Anticipatory Set: _____

_____

_____

Differentiated Learning Experiences: _____

_____

_____

Assessment and Culminating Performance: _____

_____

_____

Closure: _____

_____

_____

_____

Resources: _____ _____
_____ _____
_____ _____
_____ _____
_____ _____

Approximate Time Span: _____

CONCLUSION

This chapter has looked at best practices in teaching science to all students, as recommended by several national organizations. The list of techniques presented here is by no means exhaustive. The understanding of basic science concepts and science literacy is critical in today's world, so it is expected that additional research will be conducted to look at how educators teach science.

The lesson plan templates provided are also by no means the only desirable outlines for teaching science. You may find that you can most effectively teach science by combining strategies found in the lesson plans in this book and others that are not included. The essential ingredients are choosing topics that are relevant to students' lives; using a hands-on, discussion-based approach; asking probing questions; using a strategy or strategies that ask for a product, and finding assessments that continue the learning.

I hope that this chapter—and this book—have provided some ideas and strategies to use with not only girls, but all students. The fact that you have read this book indicates you are a teacher (or parent) interested in improving science education for youngsters. By so doing you will be improving not only the educational experience and therefore future career choices of the children with whom you interact, but also the larger sphere of individuals whom they, in turn, will influence. From one, many.

NOTES

1. Charles Coble and Michael Allen, *Keeping America Competitive: Five Strategies to Improve Math and Science Education* (Denver, CO: Education Commission of the States, 2005).
2. National Academy of Sciences, *National Science Education Standards* (Washington, DC: National Academies Press, 1996).
3. Ligaya Espaldon Avenida, "Public-Private Partnership for Education and Public Service: Toward a Globally Competitive Filipino Workforce" (paper presented at capstone lecture to the Board of Regents, Pamantasan Ng Lungsod Ng Maynila [University of the City of Manila], Manila, Philippines, November 10, 2006), 116–18.
4. Mary Ann Fitzgerald and Al Byers, "Teaching Strategies: A Rubric for Selecting Inquiry-Based Activities," at www.nsta.org/main/news/pdf/ss0209_22.pdf#search='definition%20of%20science%20inquiry' (accessed August 21, 2005). This was originally published in the September 2002 issue of *Science Scope*, the National Science Teachers Association (NSTA) professional journal for middle-school teachers.
5. Virginia Tech University, "Problem-Based Learning," at www.edtech.vt.edu/edtech/id/models/pbl.html (accessed August 21, 2005).
6. Tracey Hall, "Differentiated Instruction," at www.cast.org/publications/ncac/ncac_diffinstruc.html (accessed August 21, 2005).
7. www.free-definition.com/Constructivism-%28pedagogical%29.html (accessed August 21, 2005). [URL no longer active.—SGG.]
8. Fitzerald and Byers, "Teaching Strategies."
9. Augusta State University, at www.aug.edu/teacher_development/PBL/Elementary%20Units/Courtyard/Plants.htm (accessed September 13, 2005). [URL no longer active.—SGG.]

10. Seton Hall University, "Science Lesson Plan Format," at education.shu.edu/pt3grant/zinicola/lessonplanformat.html (accessed February 5, 2007).

11. Randolph-Macon College, "Concept-Based, Differentiated Instruction Lesson Plan Template," at faculty.rmwc.edu/mentor_grant/Differentiated/lesson_template.htm (accessed September 13, 2005).

12. San Diego State University, "Lesson Plan Formats," at edweb.sdsu.edu/Courses/EDTEC470/sections/F02-10/lesson_planning.htm (accessed September 13, 2005).

WHY THE DIFFERENCE?

*C*hapter 4 outlines five strategies for improving mathematics and science education. One of those strategies is ensuring that teachers have the knowledge and skills needed to do the job effectively. Teachers with the requisite knowledge and skills reach their students and engage their interest, foster a collaborative learning environment, and focus on activities-based, hands-on learning. That understanding underpinned the "Why the Difference?" Teachers Conference on Best Practices to Engage Girls and Students of Color in Science, Technology, Engineering, and Math that is described here. The conference was held June 27–28, 2006, at the College of St. Catherine in St. Paul, Minnesota (minerva.stkate.edu/sciencetech.nsf/), and presented by the college's Center for Women, Science and Technology. Teachers interested in follow-up experiences participated in a morning meeting on June 29. The conference was designed to build skills in teaching K–12 science, technology, engineering, and math (STEM), and it addressed how K–12 teachers can create achievement and sustained engagement in these subjects for girls and students of color, while in effect raising the achievement and engagement of all students. The motivation for this work is that few girls and students of color enter scientific and technical fields, yet demands for a technically trained workforce keep rising. The conference was supported by generous grants from the General Mills Foundation and Bigelow Foundation. The conference program is below.

Center for Women, Science and Technology. The goal of the CWST is to increase the number of women and people of color entering into STEM majors and careers. With a few exceptions, women's representation in STEM disciplines drops off dramatically when women transition from high school to college. Few people of color have strong enough skills and knowledge in STEM to be competitive in STEM fields.

CONFERENCE THEMES

- Collaborative learning
- Inquiry and activity-based learning
- Gender issues
- Real-world contexts

The conference program centered on themes of best teaching practices that relate to greater achievement in science, technology, engineering, and math. The themes were inquiry- and activity-based learning, collaborative learning, gender issues, and real-world contexts.

Nationally and locally renowned speakers introduced these topics in plenary sessions, which were followed by breakout sessions. These workshops, led mostly by faculty at colleges of education and K–12 teachers, focused on the implementation of best practices. They contained examples of implementation and opportunities for teachers to discuss new approaches.

KEYNOTE SPEAKER

Keynote speaker: Eric Jolly, PhD, president of the Science Museum of Minnesota (SMM), is known for his contributions to mathematics and science education, frequently working with such groups as the American Association for the Advancement of Science (AAAS), the National Action Council for Minorities in Engineering (NACME), the National Council for Teachers of Mathematics (NCTM), and the National Science Teachers Association (NSTA). Jolly has published many scholarly articles, including "Engagement, Capacity and Continuity: A Trilogy for Student Success," which analyzes why successful individual reform efforts have not led to broader increases in students achieving at high levels or entering science- and math-oriented careers. He is also the author of numerous books, articles, and curricula for students and teachers across the educational spectrum, including *Bridging Homes and Schools* (a comprehensive resource for teachers of Limited English Proficiency students), and *Beyond Blame: Reacting to the Terrorist Attack*. His curricula are currently used in more than sixteen countries and an estimated four hundred thousand classrooms worldwide.

ENGAGING *ALL* STUDENTS IN SCIENCE

This session was billed as "A Conversation with Patricia B. Campbell, PhD, and Angela B. Ginorio, PhD."

Campbell, president of Campbell-Kibler Associates, Inc., has been involved in educational research and evaluation with a focus on science and mathematics education and issues of race/ethnicity, gender, and disability since the mid-1970s. Campbell, who holds a PhD from Syracuse University in teacher education and is a former professor of research, measurement, and statistics at Georgia State University, has authored more than ninety publications. The publications include "Engagement, Capacity and Continuity: A Trilogy for Student Success" and "Upping the Numbers: Using Research-Based Decision Making to Increase Diversity in the Quantitative Sciences" (coauthored with Eric Jolly and Lesley Perlman), and "What Do We Know?: Seeking Effective Math and Science Education" (coauthored with Beatriz Chu Clewell). Campbell also was one of the coauthors of the AAUW report *How Schools Shortchange Girls*. Campbell was a part of the team involved in the development of the National Science Foundation publication *Infusing Equity in Systemic Reform: An Implementation Scheme*.

Ginorio is associate professor in women's studies, and adjunct associate professor in the Departments of Psychology and American Ethnic Studies at the University of Washington in Seattle. She teaches the courses Women and/in Science; Issues for Ethnic Minorities and Women in Science and Engineering; and Gendered Technologies. Her scholarship focuses on factors affecting access to and experiences in science and engineering of underrepresented groups (students and faculty of color, women, students from rural backgrounds), with particular attention to the impact of socially defined identities, parental involvement, and mentoring. She developed and directs the Rural Girls in Science Program of the University of Washington. This program, which is geared toward rural girls interested in science, teachers, counselors, parents, and community members, is designed to create an environment that is conducive to rural girls' science and math achievement. The program includes summer programs for students, teachers, and counselors; a research project during the school year; and an Internet science club.

NSF FUNDING OPPORTUNITIES

Julie Johnson, the Science Museum of Minnesota's (SMM) first John Roe Chair of Museum Leadership, delivered a presentation entitled "Funding Opportunities in Teacher Professional Development from the National Science Foundation (NSF)."

The matrix Johnson prepared for this session is illustrated in the eight tables in this appendix. Refer to these tables for a complete, and updated, matrix that she prepared. It lists NSF funding programs for science, technology, engineering, and math education and diversity, describes their scope, provides their reference numbers and website addresses, and gives query instructions for readers who want to see records of grants issued for each program listed.

In her capacity at SMM, Johnson assists the museum in furthering the implementation of its strategic plan, provides support and leadership for review of organizational and programmatic functions, facilitates the exploration and expansion of relationships and collaborations with community entities, and helps in the identification of resources to advance SMM's mission. From 2003 to 2005, she was "on loan" to the NSF, where she served as a program officer in the Elementary, Secondary and Informal Education Division. While there, she worked to fund innovative projects that support the public understanding of science, have an impact on the field of informal science education, and further what is known about learning science in informal settings. In addition, she served on the Education and Human Resources (EHR) Directorate's Internal Resource Group on Research and Evaluation. Concurrent with the assignment at NSF, Johnson was the executive vice president and chief operating officer for the New Jersey Academy for Aquatic Sciences, which operates the New Jersey State Aquarium.

PANEL: GIRLS DO SCIENCE: INCREASING ACHIEVEMENT K–12

Susan Goetz, EdD (this book's author) facilitated a panel that featured Patricia B. Campbell, PhD (Campbell-Kibler and Associates), Angela B. Ginorio, PhD (University of Washington), and Kathryn Scantlebury, PhD (University of Delaware).

Scantlebury is an associate professor of chemistry and the Secondary Science Education coordinator at the University of Delaware. In addition, she serves as a graduate faculty member of the Master of Chemistry Education Program at the University of Pennsylvania. Her research expertise is in science education with a particular focus on equity issues. Her recent activities in urban schools have extended her research on equity to include race, ethnicity, and social class as factors associated with the teaching and learning of science.

SCIENCE MUSEUM OF MINNESOTA

There was an optional evening visit to Body Worlds and other science and technology exhibits at the Science Museum of Minnesota. Body Worlds features almost two hundred authentic human specimens, revealing the anatomy of entire bodies, individual organs, and transparent body slices that have been preserved through the process of plastination, a technique that replaces bodily fluids and fat. More information is available at the museum's website: www.smm.org/bodyworlds/.

Table A.1

Scope	Name	URL*	To See Prior/Current Awards**
Research and experiments to increase participation of girls and women	Research on Gender in Science and Engineering	NSF 07-501: www.nsf.gov/funding/pgm_summ.jsp?pims_id=5475&org=HRD&from=home	Query tip: 1544
Participation and advancement of women in academic sciences and engineering careers	ADVANCE	NSF 05-584: www.nsf.gov/funding/pgm_summ.jsp?pims_id=5383&org=NSF&from=fund	Query tip: 1739, 1681, 7568
Research on underrepresentation of women and minorities in IT	IT Workforce (ITW) No longer receiving proposals; replaced by BPC (see below)	NSF 03-609: www.nsf.gov/funding/pgm_summ.jsp?pims_id=5280	Query tip: 1713 and itwf
Youth, student, and teacher programs with emphasis on information technology	Information Technology Experiences for Students and Teachers (ITEST)	NSF 07-514: www.nsf.gov/funding/pgm_summ.jsp?pims_id=5467&org=ESIE&from=home	Query tip: 7227
Out-of-school programs that link to and support in-school science learning. Youth and teacher professional development	NSF Academies for Young Scientists (NSFAYS)	NSF 06-560: www.nsf.gov/funding/pgm_summ.jsp?pims_id=13677&org=EHR&from=home	No awards yet; new as of 3/2006

* If the reference is a program announcement publication, go to www.nsf.gov/pubsys/ods/ and type in the publication number.
** To see prior and current awards, search at www.nsf.gov/awardsearch/tab.do?dispatch=2; type the number in the "element code" line and the letter code in the "search award for" field unless otherwise noted.

Table A.2

Scope	Name	URL*	To See Prior/Current Awards**
Technology Technology education, especially for two-year colleges	Advanced Technology Education (ATE)	NSF 05-530: www.nsf.gov/funding/pgm_summ.jsp?pims_id=5464&org=DUE&from=home	Query tip: 7412
Scholarship programs for talented, but financially needy undergraduate students	NSF Scholarships in Science, Technology, Engineering, and Mathematics (S-STEM)	NSF 07-524: www.nsf.gov/funding/pgm_summ.jsp?pims_id=5257&org=DUE&from=home	Query tip: 1536
Improvement of undergraduate education materials, curriculum, adaptation, and implementation of exemplary curriculum	Course, Curriculum, and Laboratory Improvement (CCLI)	NSF 06-536: www.nsf.gov/funding/pgm_summ.jsp?pims_id=5741&org=NSF	Query tip: 7431, 7428, 7493, 7427, 7494, 7429, 7492
Increase numbers of undergraduate students in STEM—planning and pilots	Science, Technology, Engineering, and Mathematics Talent Expansion Program (STEP)	NSF 06-502: www.nsf.gov/funding/pgm_summ.jsp?pims_id=5488&org=DUE&from=home	Query tip: 1796
Student scholarships and capacity building in for Service (SFS) computer security	Federal Cyber Service: Scholarship	NSF 07-512: www.nsf.gov/funding/pgm_summ.jsp?pims_id=5228&org=DUE&from=home	Query tip: 1668

* If the reference is a program announcement publication, go to www.nsf.gov/pubsys/ods/ and type in the publication number.
** To see prior and current awards, search at www.nsf.gov/awardsearch/tab.do?dispatch=2; type the number in the "element code" line and the letter code in the "search award for" field unless otherwise noted.

Table A.3

Scope	Name	URL*	To See Prior/Current Awards**
Adapt current research in learning, coordinate innovations, and serve as a resource for faculty development and comprehensive change	Centers for Learning and Teaching (in Engineering) (CLT) No longer receiving proposals; replaced by DR-K12 (see below)	NSF 05-613: www.nsf.gov/ funding/pgm_summ.jsp?pims _id=5465&org=ESIE&from= home	Query tip: 7181
Increase participation of persons with disabilities	Research in Disabilities Education (RDE)	NSF 07-511: www.nsf.gov/ funding/pgm_summ.jsp?pims _id=5482&org=HRD&from= home	Query tip: 1545
Increase production of minority students completing STEM degrees and their participation in advanced study	Alliances for Broadening Participation (ABP)	NSF 06-552: www.nsf.gov/ funding/pgm_summ.jsp?pims _id=13646&org=EHR&from= home	No awards yet
Increase production of minority students completing STEM degrees	Louis Stokes Alliances for Minority Participation (LSAMP) No longer receiving proposals; is now ABP	www.nsf.gov/pubs/2003/ nsf03520/nsf03520.htm	Query tip: 9133
Increase research capacity of minority-serving institutions	Centers of Research Excellence in Science and Technology (CREST)	NSF 07-526: www.nsf.gov/ funding/pgm_summ.jsp?pims _id=6668&org=HRD&from= home	Query tip: 9131

* If the reference is a program announcement publication, go to www.nsf.gov/pubsys/ods/ and type in the publication number.
** To see prior and current awards, search at www.nsf.gov/awardsearch/tab.do?dispatch=2; type the number in the "element code" line and the letter code in the "search award for" field unless otherwise noted.

Table A.4

Scope	Name	URL*	To See Prior/Current Awards**
Leave No Child Behind— increase capacity and reform K–12 education through large partnerships	Math and Science Partnership Program (MSP)	NSF 06-539: www.nsf.gov/ funding/pgm_summ.jsp?pims _id=5756&org=EHR&from= fund	Query tip: 1793, 1777, 1791, 1792
Improve undergraduate education in computer and information sciences and engineering by integrating research results	CISE Combined Research & Curriculum Development (CRCD) and Educational Innovation (EI)	NSF 04-001: www.nsf.gov/ funding/pgm_summ.jsp?pims _id=5458&org=NSF	Query tip: 1709
Improve pedagogy in engineering schools and develop technology-focused curricula for in-service and preservice teachers	Collaborations between schools of engineering and education; no longer receiving proposals	NSF 03-561	Query tip: 1340
Provide research experiences for undergraduates through institutional program or supplements	Research Experiences for Undergraduates (REU)	NSF 05-592: www.nsf.gov/ funding/pgm_summ.jsp?pims _id=5517&from=fund	Query tip: 9250, 9251 (in Ref. Code box)
Engage in-service and preservice teachers in engineering research	Research Experiences for Teachers (RET)	NSF 03-554 & NSF 05-524: www.nsf.gov/funding/pgm _summ.jsp?pims_id=5736& from=fund	Query tip: 1359

* If the reference is a program announcement publication, go to www.nsf.gov/pubsys/ods/ and type in the publication number.
** To see prior and current awards, search at www.nsf.gov/awardsearch/tab.do?dispatch=2; type the number in the "element code" line and the letter code in the "search award for" field unless otherwise noted.

Table A.5

Scope	Name	URL*	To See Prior/Current Awards**
Adapt current research in learning, coordinate innovations, and serve as a resource for faculty development and comprehensive change	Centers for Learning and Teaching (in Engineering) (CLT); no longer receiving proposals; replaced by DR-K12 (see below)	NSF 05-613: www.nsf.gov/funding/pgm_summ.jsp?pims_id=5465&org=ESIE&from=home	Query tip: 7181
Increase participation of persons with disabilities	Research in Disabilities Education (RDE)	NSF 07-511: www.nsf.gov/funding/pgm_summ.jsp?pims_id=5482&org=HRD&from=home	Query tip: 1545
Increase production of minority students completing STEM degrees and their participationin advanced study	Alliances for Broadening Participation (ABP)	NSF 06-552: www.nsf.gov/funding/pgm_summ.jsp?pims_id=13646&org=EHR&from=home	No awards yet
Increase production of minority students completing STEM degrees	Louis Stokes Alliances for Minority Participation (LSAMP); no longer receiving proposals; is now ABP	www.nsf.gov/pubs/2003/nsf03520/nsf03520.htm	Query tip: 9133
Increase research capacity of minority-serving institutions	Centers of Research Excellence in Science and Technology (CREST)	NSF 07-526: www.nsf.gov/funding/pgm_summ.jsp?pims_id=6668&org=HRD&from=home	Query tip: 9131

* If the reference is a program announcement publication, go to www.nsf.gov/pubsys/ods/ and type in the publication number.
** To see prior and current awards, search at www.nsf.gov/awardsearch/tab.do?dispatch=2; type the number in the "element code" line and the letter code in the "search award for" field unless otherwise noted.

Table A.6

Scope	Name	URL*	To See Prior/Current Awards**
Increase minority students' participation in advanced study	Alliances for Graduate Education and the Professoriate (AGEP); no longer receiving proposals; is now ABP	www.nsf.gov/funding/pgm_summ.jsp?pims_id=5474&org=HRD&from=fund	Query tip: 1515
Enhance quality of STEM education and increase minority undergraduate degrees	Historically Black Colleges and Universities Undergraduate Program (HBCU-UP)	NSF 06-606: www.nsf.gov/funding/pgm_summ.jsp?pims_id=5481&org=HRD&from=home	Query tip: 1594
Strengthen STEM education and numbers of undergraduate degrees	Tribal Colleges and Universities Program (TCUP)	NSF 04-602: www.nsf.gov/funding/pgm_summ.jsp?pims_id=5483&org=HRD&from=home	Query tip: 1744
Educational emphasis areas are: formal science education experiences for K–12 teachers and undergraduate or graduate students, informal science education for the broader public	International Polar Year (IPY)	NSF 06-534: www.nsf.gov/funding/pgm_summ.jsp?pims_id=13615&from=fund	Query tip: 5295, 5296, 5297, 5298, and 5299 in Ref. Code box
Research on learning; evaluation of education programs and advancing evaluation practice	Research & Evaluation on Education in Science and Engineering (REESE)	NSF 06-609: www.nsf.gov/funding/pgm_summ.jsp?pims_id=13667&org=REC&from=home	Query tip: 1666, 7180, 7261

* If the reference is a program announcement publication, go to www.nsf.gov/pubsys/ods/ and type in the publication number.
** To see prior and current awards, search at www.nsf.gov/awardsearch/tab.do?dispatch=2; type the number in the "element code" line and the letter code in the "search award for" field unless otherwise noted.

Table A.7

Scope	Name	URL*	To See Prior/Current Awards**
Supplemental funding to active BIO Division awards; promotes increased participation in the sciences	Research Assistantships for High School Students (RAHSS)	NSF 06-027: www.nsf.gov/funding/pgm_summ.jsp?pims_id=500035&org=DEB	Not searchable separately
Programs to encourage undergraduate students (especially minority) to pursue a career in environmental biology	Undergraduate mentoring in Environmental Biology (UMEB) No longer receiving proposals; replaced by URM	NSF 05-558: www.nsf.gov/funding/pgm_summ.jsp?pims_id=5450&org=DBI	Query tip: 1135
Programs to increase the number and diversity of individuals pursuing graduate studies in all areas of biological research supported by the NSF Directorate for Biological Sciences	Undergraduate Research and Mentoring in the Biological Sciences (URM)	NSF 06-591: www.nsf.gov/funding/pgm_summ.jsp?pims_id=500036&org=BIO&from=home	No awards yet
Opportunities for K–12 teachers as well as graduate, undergraduate, and doctoral students	Undergraduate Research Collaboratives (URC)	NSF 06-521: www.nsf.gov/funding/pgm_summ.jsp?pims_id=6675&org=CHE&from=home	Query tip: 1990

* If the reference is a program announcement publication, go to www.nsf.gov/pubsys/ods/ and type in the publication number.
** To see prior and current awards, search at www.nsf.gov/awardsearch/tab.do?dispatch=2; type the number in the "element code" line and the letter code in the "search award for" field unless otherwise noted.

Table A.8

Scope	Name	URL*	To See Prior/Current Awards**
Increase the number of people who are well prepared to pursue careers in the mathematical sciences	Enhancing the Mathematical Sciences Workforce in the 21st Century (EMSW21)	NSF 05-595: www.nsf.gov/funding/pgm_summ.jsp?pims_id=5732&org=DMS	Query tip: 1618, 7301, 7302 (in Ref. Code box)
Provide infrastructure that enables high-quality computing research and education; extend the set of individuals and departments able to conduct such activities	CISE Computing Research Infrastructure (CRI)	NSF 06-597: www.nsf.gov/funding/pgm_summ.jsp?pims_id=12810&org=NSF	Query tip: 2885, 7359
Diversify access to engineering research for women, minorities, and students with disabilities	Supplemental Funding for Support of Women, Minorities, and Physically Disabled Engineering Research Assistants	www.nsf.gov/od/lpa/news/publicat/nsf04009/eng/eec.htm#5	Not searchable separately
Aims to significantly increase the number of U.S. citizens and permanent residents receiving postsecondary degrees in the computing disciplines	Broadening Participation in Computing (BPC)	NSF 06-540: www.nsf.gov/funding/pgm_summ.jsp?pims_id=13510&org=CCF	Query tip: 7482

* If the reference is a program announcement publication, go to www.nsf.gov/pubsys/ods/ and type in the publication number.
** To see prior and current awards, search at www.nsf.gov/awardsearch/tab.do?dispatch=2; type the number in the "element code" line and the letter code in the "search award for" field unless otherwise noted.

SISTERS IN SCIENCE

Conference participants also were invited to take part in a forum at Minnesota Public Radio that featured Diann Jordan, author of *Sisters in Science, Conversations with Black Women Scientists on Race, Gender and Their Passion for Science*. The event began with a presentation by Jordan followed by a dialogue with audience members drawn from the scientific and technology communities. Jordan's appearance was recorded for possible radio broadcast and is being considered for C-SPAN's Book TV.

Jordan is currently a full professor of biological sciences at Alabama State University and an educational consultant. Before returning to Alabama, she worked for over ten years as a professor at the University of Missouri, Columbia. She was the first woman faculty member hired in the Department of Soil and Atmospheric Sciences, the first African American woman tenured in a research science department at the University of Missouri, Columbia (1996) and the first African American woman to earn a PhD in soil science at Michigan State University (1987). For over fifteen years, she has given seminars and workshops and written articles on the issues facing young women and minorities in science and engineering. Her articles have appeared in the leading journals as well as in magazines and newspapers. Her *Sisters in Science* is the first book of interviews with prominent black women scientists across the United States. These scientists are pioneers in their chosen scientific professions and represent a broad spectrum of disciplines, ages, and geographical locations. In the seventeen interviews, the scientists were asked a series of questions on early influences, race and gender, and strategies for success.

SESSION PRESENTERS, SESSION DESCRIPTIONS

"'Acting Up'" in Science Class" with Tim Barret and Elizabeth Karre: Science, K–6, Activity-Based Learning

Creative dramatics and storytelling techniques are demonstrated through various activities that highlight the connections between science and the arts. The Bakken Museum's senior educator and dramatist Tim Barret shows teachers how to use games and storytelling performance in the classroom to enhance their science lessons. Emphasis is placed on engaging all types of students and having these students realize that they have the innate abilities needed to perform well in science by having them demonstrate the same skills through the performing arts activities. The presentation is framed in the context of research into best practices in science education for underserved audiences by Elizabeth Murphy, special projects director at the Bakken, who holds a doctorate in physics.

"The 'Perfect' Experiment—Making Any Science Activity an Inquiry-Based Experiment" with Chris Broni: Science, K–5, Inquiry

Is inquiry too scary to try, because chaos reigns? Come discover the steps to take your students from teacher-directed labs to student-developed experiments. The session includes a hands-on opportunity to create and try your own experiment. Participants have access to teacher-developed experiment blanks and grading rubrics for use in any classroom with any science curriculum. Taught by an elementary science specialist, this presentation includes suggestions for material handling and classroom-management strategies, including creating effective lab teams.

"Facts without Memorization—Using Number Sense to Teach Addition, Subtraction, and Multiplication Facts" with Peter Brunette: Math, K–6, Activity-Based Learning

Take the drudgery out of teaching facts, and increase understanding and retention at the same time! Math feels like drudgery to kids because they spend so much time memorizing without understanding. When students learn their basic facts through memorization they forget them easily and revert to counting. Teaching students how to figure out basic facts using number sense techniques instead of memorization will help them to build thinking and problem-solving skills while learning facts, and to develop long-term retention.

"Does It Work? Making Evaluation Useful and Even Fun!" with Patricia Campbell: STEM, K–12, Research and Evaluation

In this session, participants come in with an instructional or pedagogical question that they want to answer. In this interactive session, participants receive an overview of classroom and project evaluation while they design ways to collect and analyze information from their own classrooms to answer their questions. Along with looking at ways to combine qualitative and quantitative information, participants learn how to work with students as evaluators.

"Why Don't They Hear Me? Moving Beyond Stereotypes in the Classroom" with Patricia Campbell: STEM, Grades 6–12, Gender Issues

Have you ever felt that you're shouting and no one hears; that your efforts to encourage all students in math and science are being ignored? Sex, racial, and ethnic stereotypes can have an unintentional impact on how we teach and how we are heard. In this session, participants go over what the research says makes a difference and focus on the development and adaptation of strategies to use in their own math and science classrooms.

"The R.A.F.T: Incorporating the Power of Literacy Strategies in the Science Classroom" with Yosefa Carriger: Science, Technology, and Engineering, Grades 4–12, Science and Literacy

Are you looking for a way to find out how well your students are constructing their new knowledge? Do you want to discover what latent talents your students may have while incorporating literacy in your science classroom? Are you looking for a new way to assess your students' knowledge? Do you need something fresh to review and reinforce the material learned before a test? Utilize the power of literacy to target all learning styles and intelligences in your science classroom. See how to make science relevant to your students!

"Engaging Urban Learners in Mathematics: A Social Justice Perspective" with Rose Chu: Math, Grades 4–12, Inquiry/Collaboration/Real-World Contexts

Civil rights leader Robert Moses says, "The absence of math literacy in urban and rural communities throughout this country is an issue as urgent as the lack of Black voters in Mississippi was in 1961." Come experience mathematics from a social justice perspective, which is a viable and arguably necessary approach to engage urban learners.

"The Area Model: From Combining Like Terms to Factoring and Beyond" with Lisa Comfort and Cheryl Tucker: Math, Grades 7–12, Activity-Based Learning

Come see how algebra tiles can make some abstract concepts more tangible and understandable for your learners. Participants experience how the area model can scaffold learning for students from prealgebra concepts through algebra 2 material, making mathematics more accessible and understandable to students.

"Incorporating Visualization and Language in Early Math" with Joan Cotter: Math, Grades K–3, Activity-Based Learning

Research shows that visualizing quantities, not counting, helps children develop number sense. Even infants visualize small quantities. Children in Japan are discouraged from counting for adding or subtracting; they learn to visualize by using a subbase of 5. Also discussed are the advantages of the "math way" for number naming. Learn how visual strategies help children master the facts.

"Using a Visual Model to Teach Fractions" with Joan Cotter: Math, Grades 4–6, Activity-Based Learning

Fractions are a gateway to many middle-school topics, including division, decimals, ratio, proportion, measurement, probability, and formulas. A linear model makes it possible to visualize fractions. It also enables fractions to be greater than one, a very important attribute that circles do not allow. This session discusses the linear model and demonstrates some new techniques, including simplifying fractions on the multiplication chart and multiplying fractions visually. The problems of methods used in older textbooks are discussed.

"Learning Geometry with a Drawing Board and Tools" with Joan Cotter: Math, Grades 4–8, Activity-Based Learning

Students love to use drawing boards, T squares, and triangles to construct geometrical figures, including equilateral triangles, hexagons, stars, squares, and tangrams; and to discover the the relationships between these figures. This work naturally blends with fractions, measurement, area, symmetry, and art. These methods and tools form the basis of the CAD (computer-aided design) software programs that designers and engineers use to construct their drawings.

"Using Action Research to Assess for and Improve All Student Learning" with Milo Cutter: Grades K–12, Research and Evaluation

For the past seven years, City Academy has used Action Research as a tool for improving student learning, schoolwide improvement, and staff development. The session presents the rationale for implementing Action Research and the results experienced at City Academy.

"A Coloring Activity to Teach Basic Mechanical Concepts" with Roz Dolid: Engineering, Grades 4–6, Activity-Based Learning

Coloring is an activity that attracts some people. This particular activity involves coloring in parts of a bicycle, learning the part names, and discussing their basic functionality. The presentation leader is a role model for the students; she teaches fundamental mechanical concepts and describes various engineering careers that relate to bicycles. This activity combines auditory, visual, and tactile learning styles into one package.

"Biotechnology—Curriculum and Skill Sets" with Rekha Ganaganur, Phil Gerlach, and Krista Benjamin: Science, Grades 9–12; Inquiry, Real-World Contexts

The bioscience industry is growing in Minnesota and in the nation. There is a need at all education levels for training programs in bioscience that will provide skilled employees in this field. This session provides insight into skill sets and competencies required for entry-level positions and the resources, made available through national centers such as Biotechnology Institute and Bio-Link, for incorporating biotechnology into the curriculum.

"Explore Careers in Science" with facilitator Simone Gbolo: Science, Grades 9–12, Real-World Contexts

A research scientist, regulatory affairs specialists from biomedical device firms, a professor of biochemistry, and a CEO of a biomedical device company describe their research and projects in order to help teachers convey to students how science is studied or applied in business and academia.

"Peer into Engineering Careers" with facilitator Simone Gbolo: Engineering, Grades 9–12, Real-World Contexts

A civil engineer, a mechanical engineer, a sensory engineer, an environmental analyst, and a project manager from academia and industry describe their research and projects in order to help teachers convey to students how engineering projects take place in business and academia.

"Insight into Applied Math and Technology Careers" with facilitator Simone Gbolo: Math and Technology, Grades 9–12, Real-World Contexts

An actuary, a biostatistician, and a biotechnologist present on applied-math and technology careers in order to help teachers convey to students how math is applied in technology positions.

"Science in the Community: Long-Term Research Projects" with Angela Ginorio, Robert Johnson, and Oladele Gazal (double session): Science, Grades 9–12, Inquiry

In this two-part interactive session participants become familiar with the components of a long-term research project (LTRP) initiated by high-school students and facilitated by their teachers. The five LTRP components are: connection to students' interests and communities, focus on the scientific process, expert resources, noncompetitive collaboration, and support from adults in the students' lives (teachers, families, and community members).

"Environmental Science at Carleton—A Successful Model Summer Program Targeted at Traditionally Underrepresented High-School Students and Science Teachers" with Bill Holden and Todd Olson

Environmental Science at Carleton brings together between eighteen and twenty-four mainly urban high-school students of color and six to eight high-school teachers to work on collaborative research projects with Carleton faculty and community partners. In small groups led by the teachers, students research a specific topic, hypothesize about the possible outcomes, collect and analyze data, and then synthesize their findings into a public poster and oral presentation session. Alumni statistics show excellent college admission outcomes from this program, and alumni report an easier transition between high school and college.

"Using Technology in a Science Classroom to Investigate Real-World Problems" with Clayton Holt: Science, Technology, Grades 6–12, Real-World Contexts

Teachers see how technology can be used in the classroom to investigate global warming. Global warming is an ideal topic for teaching science: the consequences of global warming are still uncertain; the topic contains many important science concepts; and global warming may have large social as well as economic impact worldwide. Predictions gathered by scientists on global warming can be found in the media on a daily basis. Using a global climate model (GCM) to learn about global warming supplies students with the same type of technology that a scientist might use in problem solving. Furthermore, the computer allows studies of science concepts that cannot be performed easily in the lab.

"Putting History into Science: Making Science "Real" to Our Students" with Diann Jordan: Science and History, Grades K-12, Gender Issues, Real-World Contexts

Are you having a hard time getting your students interested in science or caring about who Gregor Mendel, Charles Darwin, or Rosalind Franklin were? Would your students recognize the names Ruth Ella Moore, Georgia Dunston, Ernest Just, or Alexa Canady? Let's make science and the scientist more "real" to our students. This session focuses on using biographies and interviews to give students a more "real" picture of the scientist behind the science. The session is interactive. The presenter begins the session with a fun history quiz on scientists with emphasis on scientists of color. Sample assignments using biographies and interviews are presented in the session. The African American woman scientist's history is used as a model to stimulate the discussion. If time permits, mock interviews are done among the participants to help formulate and modify questions that will be useful for students at a particular grade level. The session is geared to the high-school grades but any teacher might find it useful.

"Science, Engineering, and Technology in the Math Classroom" with Denise Kapler: STEM, Grades 6-8, Inquiry, Activity-Based Learning

This is an overview of various topics to bring into a middle-school math class to provide a connection to the sciences, engineering, and technology. Class participants are actively involved in this learning. Proportional reasoning provides the theme as they explore such areas as structures, rockets, automotive design, and motion.

"Moving through the Cartesian Coordinate System" with Denise Kapler: STEM, Grades 6-8, Inquiry, Activity-Based Learning

Through aerobics, dance, and other up-and-out-of-your-desk activities, participants move and groove to the beat of the coordinates. The emphasis is on focusing the energy of students on learning algebraic reasoning through the use of the patterns, the number line, and graphing. Participants explore such topics as Hooke's law, solutions, Zeno's paradox, and Fibonacci numbers.

"Probing Science with Computers" with Sherri Kreuser: Science, Technology, Grades 6-12, Inquiry, Activity-Based Learning

Participants get involved with using Vernier probes, LoggerPro software, and laptop computers as they carry out science experiments. These experiments include endothermic and ectothermic reactions and the monitoring of blood pressure and heart rate. Participants collect the data and analyze it using graphs developed with LoggerPro.

"Best Practices for Field Days: Guidelines and Tools for Creating Engaging STEM Programs" with Nate Meyer: Science, Technology, Grades 4-6, Inquiry

The University of Minnesota Extension Service *Best Practices for Field Days: A Program Planning Guidebook for Organizers, Presenters, Teachers and Volunteers* applies research and experience to provide tips and tools for planning conservation field days, environmental fairs, and similar programs. In this session, participants explore the guidelines with focus on using the Experiential Learning Model, place-based education, and other methods to design engaging programs for multicultural students, girls, and students of color.

"Global Learning and Observations to Benefit the Environment Program" with Anthony Murphy and Susan Goetz: Science, Grades 4–12, Inquiry, Activity-Based Learning

Global Learning and Observations to Benefit the Environment (GLOBE) is a worldwide hands-on, primary- and secondary-school-based education and science program. Participants hear about GLOBE programs in schools and engage in hands-on atmosphere protocols involving GPS, clouds, air and temperature, and precipitation on the St. Kate's site.

"Physics Day: Health-Care Educators Partnering with High Schools" with Susan Nelson: Science, Grades 9–12, Real-World Contexts

This session explores the development of a partnership between an urban high school and allied health-care educators. One highlight of the partnership is an annual Physics Day in which a diverse group of high-school students is welcomed to the college and exposed to various physics concepts as they apply to different medical practices. These concepts are presented using interactive problem-solving methods. Health-care programs involved are encouraged to invite their own students to assist in the activities.

"Putting the U into Groups" with Fawnda Norman: Math, Grades 6–12, Collaborative Learning

This session focuses on working with collaborative groups in a classroom setting. Topics include how to assign groups, how to set up the groups, how to manage the group work, and how to keep the groups motivated while working. These techniques have been used at the high-school and middle-school levels with regular, advanced, and at-risk students.

"Why Engineering? What Engineering Can Do for Your Curriculum" with Yvonne Ng: Engineering, Grades 4–8, Real-World Contexts

What is engineering and how can you relate it to what you are teaching now? How can you teach it to fifth through eighth graders when most introductory engineering courses are taught in the second or third year of college? This session presents findings from the College of St. Catherine course INDI 111: Engineering in Your World, has participants experience some activities, and shows how to use engineering projects to connect multiple aspects of your students' curriculum.

"Female-Friendly Science" with Patricia Paulson: Science, Grades 4–12, Gender Issues

The traditional reality of predominantly white, Western male scientists has discouraged many women and minorities from pursuing careers in science. While many have blamed this phenomenon on the lack of female and minority role models, research now demonstrates more subtle factors affecting the continued disparities within the field. The session focuses primarily on female-friendly science, but in most instances the content can be applied to all classrooms.

"Using Better Questions to Promote Inquiry; with Patricia Paulson: Science, Grades 4–6, Inquiry

The heart of inquiry is asking good questions to engage learners, but research demonstrates that most questions teachers ask are of a lower, knowledge-only level. This session involves participants in rethinking questioning strategies in order to encourage learners to think more deeply about science investigations as well as to design their own investigations. The importance of pre-thinking good questions prior to instruction is emphasized. Sample inquiry lessons are used to practice question development.

"Coteaching as Professional Development in Science" with Kathryn Scantlebury: Science, Grades 9–12

For several years, cooperating teachers have cotaught science with their student teachers and inclusion teachers. This session addresses how teachers and student teachers use coteaching in high-school classes to critically analyze teaching and learning and improve practice to enhance student learning. In coteaching, learning to teach occurs as praxis and the coteachers are aware of some of what they learn, while much of what is learned happens without awareness.

"Using Cogenerative Dialogues to Bring Girls into Science" with Kathryn Scantlebury: Science, Grades 9–12, Gender Issues

For several years, teachers in urban schools have used cogenerative dialogues as an approach to engage their students in conversations about the teaching and learning of science. This session addresses how teachers and students use cogenerative dialogues in high-school classes to provide female students with a voice, to establish collective responsibility and agency for the teaching and learning, to restructure power relations, and to challenge ideologies about science by engaging underrepresented students.

"Design and Implementation of Pedagogies of Engagement: with Karl Smith: STEM, Grades K–12, Collaboration

How can we structure our courses to ensure that they lead to enhanced learning? How can the Understanding by Design approach developed by Wiggins and McTighe assist us in our planning? Participants in this interactive workshop explore the teacher's role in designing and structuring Pedagogies of Engagement to create high-quality learning environments for students. Research insights from "How People Learn" and cooperative learning are highlighted.

"Proof! Finally a Logical Approach!" with Cheryl Tucker and Lisa Comfort: Math, Grades 9–12, Inquiry and Activity-Based Learning

The development of proof begins with deductive reasoning by way of games. Using reasoning skills, students begin by justifying their thinking both orally and in writing to support their solutions to such logic games as the three- and four-color squares. The goal is to use communication, reasoning, and logic as a lead-in to developing formal proofs in geometry. Students also employ both inductive and deductive reasoning to write conjectures using hands-on investigations and activities.

"Jump-Starting Improvement with Collaborative Action Research" with Kenneth Vos: STEM, Grades K-12, Research and Evaluation

Collaborative action research is a process by which educators use the techniques of research to examine their own practice systematically and carefully. This session reviews the basic tenets of action research within a classroom setting. After a brief overview of action research, participants explore with one another potential collaborative action research investigations. This process includes the reflective interview, analytic discourse, and graphical representation components.

"Developing Algebraic Thinking" with Terry Wyberg: Math, Grades 7-12

This session demonstrates several activities that encourage algebraic thinking by helping students make connections between various representations. Participants learn how questioning can be used to successfully focus student learning on algebraic ideas.

FOLLOWING UP

Teachers with keen interest in building new teaching skills had the opportunity to stay engaged with the project into the 2006–2007 year. A committee of program staff, College of St. Catherine faculty, visiting professors, an evaluator, and ten teachers from ten school districts met four times following the conference to develop a research agenda to refine and substantiate best practices. The meetings of the second year presented a fabulous opportunity to work alongside experts in STEM teaching.

In addition, several teachers, or teams of teachers, engaged in action research about a best practice to help refine the research questions. Action research is process of research design, data collection, and data analysis for evaluating effectiveness of a teaching technique. Teachers interested in a master's degree would find this experience very beneficial.

B

HOW HANDS-ON, MINDS-ON METHODS WORK
An A+ Way of Teaching Science

A few years back, British Petroleum (BP) created its A+ for Energy program and competition to recognize educators whose efforts help children learn about energy and energy conservation. Mitzie Romero, who came to the United States from the Philippines to teach in 2001, thought hers was a good enough project to take a shot at a prize.

She hit the jackpot. Romero received a $10,000 honorarium and an invitation to the 2005 National Energy Education Development (NEED) Conference for Educators, a NEED Science of Energy Kit, and student materials. (The NEED Project, founded in 1980, provides energy education training and curriculum to K–12 teachers and students throughout the United States. It is dedicated to promoting a realistic understanding of the scientific, economic, and environmental impacts of energy.)

Recognizing that teachers set the standard of excellence in education, Irene Brown, director of California community relations for the oil company, wrote to tell Romero, "It is teachers like you who provide innovative and motivating experiences that deepen children's knowledge about energy and energy conservation."

The winning teacher works at an alternative high school in the Sacramento (California) City Unified School District. Her winning project is an ongoing initiative that is proving effective in developing desirable skills, positive attitudes and values toward self-motivation, redirection, and sound decision making among the "highly at-risk" student population she teaches. (To get an idea of what highly at-risk means in Romero's context, consider that the project gave her pupils an opportunity to prove their potential to their parents and the community—and their probation officers.)

Romero's award-winning effort is a multidisciplinary project-based learning (PBL) program that employs innovative hands-on and "minds-on" activities about energy awareness, conservation, and use.

For teachers and students alike, energy seems to be an ideal subject for integrating real-life applications within the classroom and tying them into the core curriculum. Energy education can be an exciting way to stimulate students, help them absorb valuable content, and let them discover how knowledge about energy enriches other subject areas.

Synthesizing and supporting what they learn takes students into realms that surpass pure science and enter language, performing arts, social studies, math, and other subjects. For instance, students learn the geography of energy resources and how these resources are recovered for use. They develop plans to increase electricity capacity in a developing country, taking into account the implications for the economy, the environment, and the society. They debate advantages and disadvantages of various energy sources while honing critical analysis skills. They write slogans, poems, and essays about energy. They design posters. They compose "energy jingles."

They create and perform "energy rap." Discussing a variety of fuels (such as gasoline, diesel, ethanol, biodiesel, propane, CNG, and methanol), they compare and contrast the fuels, weigh the pros and cons, evaluate the status today, and explore the potential for tomorrow.

In addition to extending their horizons in considering global implications of energy issues, the students also pick up some good life skills that link the lessons to their daily lives. For instance, they learn about caulk, weather stripping, and programmable thermostats. They learn to evaluate information from EnergyGuide labels on appliances. They learn how to read meters to monitor energy consumption as they look for ways to reduce, reuse, and recycle.

Of course, students learn the science of energy—heat, light, motion, sound, nuclear energy, and electricity—with hands-on explorations that emphasize the scientific process and experimental design. Taking the "hands-on, minds-on" approach, they build batteries and electromagnets, cook in solar ovens, and make compasses. Romero's students even designed a solar-powered automobile for the Solar Car Assemble 'n' Race Contest.

While younger students have fun with energy by drilling for oil in cupcakes, mining coal from chocolate chip cookies, and electrolyzing water to produce the hydrogen that may one day fuel their vehicles, the adolescents dig more deeply. They delve into fusion and fission, photovoltaics and superconductors, green pricing, and politics. They consider clean-coal technologies, renewables, and natural gas cogeneration. They research nuclear energy as an option for generating the nation's electricity. They explore transportation options to learn more about biodiesel, ethanol, gasoline, and hydrogen fuel cells. They also learn about:

- Atoms and the particles that make up atoms
- Electrons and how they move
- Fuel cells that can provide uninterrupted power to buildings
- Conduction, convection, vibration, reflection, refraction, and energy generation

To sustain energy awareness, the school maintains a year-round A+ for Energy showcase. It features student-made projects such as laminated posters on various renewable and nonrenewable sources of energy, graphic organizers, writings, a vocabulary box, energy magazines, books, and brochures. The showcase also houses a portfolio that depicts an array of student involvement and engagement activities. These all became avenues for many students to show they can succeed if given the appropriate learning environments and experiences. Because the program sparks their creativity and engages their minds, students emerge from their involvement more confident, more scientifically savvy, and better equipped to make more informed decisions as they move on with their lives.

SINGLE-SEX SCHOOLS: YEA OR NAY?
Challenging the System

ASSUMPTIONS AND DATA BEHIND THE PUSH FOR SINGLE-SEX SCHOOLING

Information in this section is reprinted with permission of Patricia B. Campbell, Ph.D., president, Campbell-Kibler Associates, Inc., and Jo Sanders, director, Center for Gender Equity, Washington Research Institute.[1]

- "It's kind of nice not to have guys here." —Fourteen-year-old student at a girls' school (*Washington Times*, June 2, 1999)
- The girls in the all-girls algebra class "are in a risk-free environment, supportive rather than competitive." —Curriculum director (*Philadelphia Inquirer*, October 14, 1998)
- "If [my daughter] wants to be president of the country, who am I to ruin her chances by having her overshadowed by some boy?" —Mother of a kindergartner in a girls' school (*New York Times*, April 11, 1999)

For decades, coeducation has been the norm for K–12 public education in the United States. Beginning in the 1980s, however, well-publicized reports that girls were being shortchanged in schools and that coeducation provides a "chilly climate" for women and girls (Bailey et al. 1992; Hall and Sandler 1982) and popular books such as *Reviving Ophelia* (Pipher 1994) and *Failing at Fairness* (Sadker and Sadker 1994) began to refuel an interest in the education girls were receiving. The reports and books called for reducing the impact of gender bias and stereotyping in education and for improving the education of girls and of boys.

But many who read about gender issues in schools and reflected on their own and their daughters' education appeared to conclude that healthy coeducation for girls was extremely difficult to achieve, and that single-sex education was a much more feasible solution. A 1998 survey of the National Coalition of Girls' Schools found applicants to their member schools increased by a third in the previous seven years, and enrollments increased by nearly a fifth (NCGS 1998).

As part of this trend, new girls-only schools have been established, including the Julia Morgan Middle School for Girls in Oakland, California, which opened its doors in 1999; the Young Women's Leadership Charter School in Chicago in 2000; and the Seattle Girls' School in 2001, the latter two focusing on math, science, and technology.

Underlying this increased interest in single-sex education for girls has been a variety of claims for the superiority of single-sex education over coeducation for girls. There are claims for girls' superior academic achievement, participation in math, science, and technology, happiness, and better careers resulting from the single-sex environment. Are the claims valid? This chapter will cast a critical look at the assumptions and the research behind the view of single-sex schooling as the answer to girls' educational problems. In so doing, we will consider public and private schooling from kindergarten through college.

WHAT DO RESEARCHERS SAY?

There has been no national comprehensive controlled study of academic performance for U.S. students in public and private K–12 single-sex and coed schooling.[2] Such a study has been conducted, however, at the college level. Looking at U.S. colleges and universities, Astin (1993) found that whether a college was coed, single-sex female, or predominantly male[3] had no meaningful effect on a variety of areas including standardized measures of general knowledge, communication skills, or professional knowledge. Neither were there differences in terms of critical thinking, analytic or problem-solving skills, writing skills, foreign language skills, public speaking ability, job skills, or preparation for professional or graduate school.

Having a greater proportion of women administrators or faculty members in a college did have a positive impact on women's education (Astin 1993), as did having a learning environment, which validated women's scholarship and women's issues (Sax 1994). Indeed, such a positive learning environment had a stronger effect on women's achievement than having more women or a greater proportion of female students in a major (Sax 1994).

At the precollege level in the United States, no work has been done with a nationally representative public school sample because there are very few public single-sex environments—either classes or schools, due to Title IX and other possible legal constraints.[4] However, some studies examining individual schools or other single-sex educational environments have been done in the United States as well as in Australia and Great Britain. The results of these studies are not consistent. For example, in studies of achievement and continuation in math and science course taking, one study found no differences in girls' subsequent math and science course taking based on whether they have been in single-sex or coed classes (Wood and Brown 1997), while another found short-term but not long-term gain (Leder and Forgasz 1994). No differences in grades or SAT scores between girls in single-sex math classes and those in coed classes were reported by some researchers (Gilson 1999; Wood and Brown 1997), while other researchers found single-sex groupings had little effect on the achievement scores of either males or females (Parker 1985; Leder and Forgasz 1994). Still another study (Smith 1986) identified short-term but not long-term achievement gains for girls in single-sex classes over girls in coed classes (Campbell and Wahl 1998b).

Using national data sets, there has been research done across representative samples of Catholic and other private schools in the United States, where there are enough single-sex institutions to make the analysis valid. Using a national sample of Catholic schools, studies done by Valerie Lee and her colleagues (e.g., Lee and Bryk 1986, 1989; Lee and Marks 1990) documented benefits for girls in single-sex schooling, but generally found few differences in the relative benefits of single-sex and coeducational schooling for boys (Lee 1998, 43). Le-Pore and Warren (1996), however, found that single-sex Catholic secondary schools were not particularly advantageous academic settings compared to coed Catholic secondary schools and that the few observed advantages of attending Catholic single-sex schools benefited boys more than girls.

When Lee and her colleagues replicated her work on Catholic secondary schools using a national sample of independent (private, not Catholic) high schools (Lee and Marks 1992; Lee, Marks, and Byrd 1994), they found "no consistent pattern of effects for attending either single-sex or coeducational independent schools for either girls or boys" (Lee 1998, 43). Based on his earlier work on Catholic secondary schools, Riordan (1990) concluded that the relative impact of single-sex and coeducational schools was "virtually zero for middle-class or otherwise advantaged students" but was significant for at-risk students, although these effects are "small in comparison with the much larger effects of home background and type of curriculum in a given school" (Riordan 1998, 54).

Riordan's conclusion about the size of the effect due to the single-sex versus coed nature of the school points out a problem with much of the research on single-sex education and provides one explanation as to why the results are inconsistent. Many of the studies of single-sex education do not control for such important variables as the curriculum, student self-selection, or even the teacher. When, for example, single-sex classes taught by one or more teachers are compared to coed classes taught by different teachers, there is no way of telling what proportion of any difference found is due to the teacher and how much is due to the sex breakdown of the class. This is an especially important caveat in view of the research on the importance of the teacher's role in the classroom, and how much the quality and experience of teachers is related to their students' achievement (Wenglinsky 2000).

The content, practice, and organization of an educational setting matter greatly when student achievement is being assessed, as do the climate and the culture, so it is curious that these factors have been secondary considerations in the research when they have been addressed at all. Yet too much of the literature and discussion compares schools providing different levels of content and pedagogy, and yet concludes that differences are due to the schools' sex composition (Campbell and Wahl 1998a).

As the U.S. Department of Education's 1993 special report on single-sex schools reminded readers, "All single-gender schools are not equal in providing a productive learning environment and many factors contributing to the success to effective single-gender schools are fundamental to effective schools regardless of their gender policy—a small student body, strong emphasis on academics and commitment to the schools' mission and value" (Hollinger 1993, 11). Gill (1996, 16) agrees, feeling that "[a]ll of the research around the topic of single-sex schooling compared with coeducation skirts some highly significant issues to do with what actually happens in one or the other type of schooling. The issue of gender difference in learning outcomes appears more as a question of classroom treatments and teacher expertise than of school gender context per se."

As Campbell and Wahl (1998b, 63) pointed out, "While the question 'Are single-sex classes better than coed classes?' may sound logical, it makes little sense when there is no consideration of what goes on in the classes, the pedagogy and practices of the teachers, or anything about the students other than their sex. Yet the public, media, educators, and even some researchers compare classes and attribute outcomes to this single factor of whether the class is all girls, all boys, or girls and boys together. Imagine how parents would respond if asked if they would prefer that their child attend a good single-sex math class or a bad coed math class, versus a bad single-sex math class or a good coed one. Basically, single-sex schooling and coeducational schooling can each be highly effective, ineffective, or somewhere in the middle."

That said, there can be much to learn from highly effective all-girl schools, at least in terms of girls' attitudes toward schooling. In a survey of over 4,000 graduates of girls' schools in the United States (National Coalition of Girls' Schools 2000), 85 percent rated their schools as very good or excellent. Something positive is going on there and it would be worth our while to learn what that might be.

WHAT DEFINES SINGLE-SEX SCHOOLING?

The degree to which confounding variables are accounted for is one reason for unclear and often contradictory results in research on single-sex education, but another equally important reason is that while we may think we know what the phrase "single-sex schooling" means, the phrase signifies several mutually contradictory things to different people.

"Single-sex schooling has been seen, simultaneously, as both conservative and progressive, and as both oppressive and empowering" (Parker and Rennie 1996, 1). Supporting single-sex education are conservatives such as columnists John Leo and George Will, educators such as Diane Ravitch, and even the *Wall Street Journal*. Also supporting it are feminists and feminist organizations such as columnist and lawyer Susan Estrich, researcher Catherine Krupnick, and Girls Incorporated.

Feminists supporting single-sex schooling often see it as the best means for girls and boys to achieve equal educational outcomes and find it an appropriate response to perceived different learning styles and maturation rates of boys and girls. They also feel it can provide young people with an environment free from the distractions and harassment often posed by the presence of the opposite sex. Conservatives, meanwhile, often support single-sex education as the best strategy for maintaining essential differences between girls and boys. To them, education should be linked to preserving different roles based on gender (Parker and Rennie 1996; Campbell and Wahl 1998a).[5]

The range of definitions of and justifications for single-sex education should not be surprising. Traditionally single-sex environments have been established for a variety of reasons, ranging from ultrafeminist to ultraconservative. Some colleges, such as Smith College and Mount Holyoke College, were established with the specific mission of empowering women and advancing their careers, and they continue to adhere to this mission. Many of the newly established all-girls grade schools have also been set up with overtly feminist missions.

We must not forget, though, that other single-sex environments have been established with quite different goals in mind. Some, such as some women's clubs and societies, were established with educational, political, social, health, and/or special interest (e.g., gardening) goals and do not deal with gender issues. Other single-sex organizations, such as ladies' auxiliaries, have as their goal the support of their men's activities. Still other all-female environments, such as purdah, have as their goal to keep women "pure" and to guard men from "temptation" by keeping women separate and secluded. [The practice of preventing men from seeing women that is most evident in Islamic and Indian communities, purdah may take the form of either physical segregation of the sexes or of requiring women to cover their bodies so as to cover their skin and conceal their shape—or it may take both forms together. —SGG.]

That single-sex environments, particularly single-sex education, can mean different things to different people is emphasized by the recent experience of California's single-sex academies. In 1997, the state of California funded six pairs of public single-sex schools, intended as "magnet schools for at-risk students" (Bennett 1997). To address legal concerns, particularly those raised by Title IX, each pair of schools was required to offer the same resources and opportunities to students. In a recent report, Datnow and her colleagues learned, based on hundreds of interviews with people involved in the academies, that participation in single-sex schooling was not a means to either a feminist or a conservative education, but was for most administrators a source of available cash for the purpose of "meeting at-risk students' needs" (Datnow, Hubbard, and Woody 2001, 5). There was no attention to gender bias and teachers did not receive professional development on gender-equitable educational practices. As a perhaps predictable result, "traditional gender stereotypes were often reinforced" (Datnow, Hubbard, and Woody 2001, 7).

It may just be, as Heather Johnson Nicholson has pointed out, that "whether a separate, or single-sex, setting for girls is especially positive for girls or promotes gender equity depends very much on the environment, values and relationships established there" (Nicholson 1992, 42).

WHY IS SINGLE-SEX SCHOOLING SO OFTEN SEEN AS THE ANSWER?

With ambiguous and contradictory research results about single-sex and coeducational schooling, increasing acknowledgement of the many variables that have an impact on girls' and boys' educational experiences and the variety of often conflicting goals for single-sex education, the question now becomes, Why is single-sex schooling so often seen as the answer? The following provides an overview of some of the answers to that question as well as an exploration of related research and justifications for each of those answers.

Assumption #1

Girls and boys are viewed as having different skills, interests, and learning styles; thus, they are better served by single-sex schooling.

This rationale for single-sex education is popular but it is not accurate. Most of us—educators or not—tend to assume that girls and boys are different, that they are indeed "opposite sexes."[6] In this dichotomous view we see girls as one way, boys as another, as in "boys are competitive, girls are cooperative." There is great diversity among girls and among boys. Indeed, other than primary sex characteristics, differences *within* girls as a group and within boys as a group are much, much larger than differences *between* girls as a group and boys as a group (Willingham and Cole 1997; Maccoby and Jacklin 1974).[7] Knowing that a person is female does not tell us if her athletic ability is closer to the Williams sisters or a couch potato. Knowing that a person is male tells us nothing about whether his math skills reflect those of an Einstein or a "mathphobe" (Sanders and Campbell 2001).

Researchers have known for many years that the differences among boys and among girls are far greater than any differences between an "average" girl and an "average" boy (Willingham and Cole 1997; Bailey et al. 1992). Analyses of thousands of studies have found that gender differences in cognitive and affective areas are actually quite small. For example, the degree of overlap in girls' and boys' math skills has been found to be between 98 and 99 percent, while in verbal skills the degree of overlap has been found to be about 96 percent (Hyde, Fennema, and Lamon 1990; Hyde and Linn 1988). As the press release headlined about a recent book on gender and assessment, there are "more gender similarities than differences in educational performance" (Educational Testing Service 1997, 1). There are many boys who learn better in the cooperative, relational styles commonly associated with girls' learning style, and many girls who learn better in the competitive individualistic style often associated with boys (Campbell and Wahl 1998a).

Assumption #2

Our efforts to reduce the gender gaps in subjects such as math and science, or in promoting coed environments that serve both boys and girls, have not been successful. Thus, single-sex classes are the only option left for addressing the inequities.

In the past twenty years there have been major advances in girls' math and science achievement and course taking. There are now minimal differences in girls' and boys' average science and math scores on the fourth-, eighth-, and twelfth-grade National Assessment of Educational Progress tests (NAEP) (National Science Foundation 1999). Girls are now taking upper-level math and science courses needed to enter college majors in these areas in about the same numbers as boys. Today, over 40 percent of high school physics and calculus students are girls, although girls remain dramatically underrepresented in Advanced Placement physics and computer science courses (American College Testing 1998; National Science Foundation 1999).

Women have the ability and the basic academic background needed to continue on in science, engineering, and technology equal to men but they are not going into those fields in anywhere near the numbers men are (National Science Foundation 2000; Thom 2001). For many girls, *interest* in these areas is not there. By eighth grade, in all racial/ethnic groups, twice as many boys as girls say they are interested in careers in the physical sciences, engineering, and technology. Girls were found to have less interest in math than boys and less confidence in their math abilities, even though they don't lag behind boys in grades or test scores (Catsambis 1995).[8]

Studies of graduates of women's colleges found these students were more likely than women from coed colleges to continue on in the natural sciences (Tidball and Kistiakowsky 1976). However, reanalysis of those data controlling for variables such as socioeconomic status found that attending a women's college had minimal impact on whether a female student continued on in the sciences (Crosby et al. 1994). Other studies carried out on women students enrolled in college after Title IX was implemented, when almost all colleges and universities were open to women, have tended not to find career differences between women in women's colleges and those in coed colleges (Astin 1993), although Riordan (1992) found women from women's colleges more apt to be in "higher prestige jobs."

It is instructive to see what happened when a private boys' school and a private girls' school in the western United States both recently decided to go coed but remain separate. Before coeducation, the girls' school offered a variety of mathematics courses at the lower end of the curriculum, while the boys' school offered more upper-division mathematics. As the authors explained, after coeducation the faculty members of the boys' school "did not change the academic or the extra-curricular programs when females entered the school because they believed they already had the best curriculum." However, as males entered Grove High School [a pseudonym for the former girls' school] "many changes occurred in the academic programs, curriculum, and extra-curricular offerings," Grove administrators even changed its name, originally St. Theresa of the Grove (again a pseudonym), because it was felt that such a feminine name would not be attractive to boys. "As a school originally designed for girls, Grove was *not* good enough for boys" (Brody et al. 2000, 88–89, 100; emphasis in the original).

Coeducation has successfully reduced gender gaps in math and science achievement and course participation but not in interest in the subjects or continuation into related careers. However, it is not clear that single-sex education would do any better.

Assumption #3

Single-sex schooling provides girls with leadership opportunities they would not get in coed environments.

All-girl schools are seen as guaranteeing leadership opportunities that are presumed to go to males in coed schools. There is some data to support this assumption. In coed schools many more girls than boys *participate* in student government and most other extracurricular activities, with the exception of athletics (National Center for Education Statistics 2000, table 147; Dwyer and Johnson 1997).

However, the pattern is different when it comes to *leadership positions* in these activities. Even though girls are much more likely to be in honor societies, music groups, service organizations, and academic groups (e.g., art, computer, debate) boys are somewhat more apt to be in leadership positions within the organizations. Girls are more apt to be in leadership positions in literary activities (e.g., yearbook, newspaper) and slightly more apt to be leaders in career groups (e.g., future teachers, future farmers) and student government (Dwyer and Johnson 1997). Leadership opportunities are apparently opening up to girls in coed schools.

Assumption #4

Single-sex schooling is not about money; money is spent equally on girls and boys' schools.

Money and the resources it buys have always been an issue in single-sex education. "Separate but equal" has always been a myth in American education. At the college level, the lack of equitable or equivalent resources between the all-male and the all-female colleges was a major reason for the U.S. Supreme Court's decision that women must be admitted into the Virginia Military Academy (VMI) (United States 1997). Expert witness analysis of VMI and its sister school, Mary Baldwin College, and of the Citadel in South Carolina and its sister school, Converse College, by the first coauthor, found major differences in the all-male and all-female institutions. The men of VMI and the Citadel had many more resources and hence opportunities than did the women of Mary Baldwin and Converse, including more sports, more athletic facilities, more academic majors, more computers, and even more library books. The resources and opportunities that were offered were stereotyped, as well as unequal. For example, the Citadel offered degrees in engineering and had a sports stadium seating over 22,000 people. Converse offered degrees in music and art and had a concert hall seating 1,500 (Campbell 1995). Such differences are not limited to these four schools. Smith College recently became the first and still the only women's college in the country to have an engineering department and offer an engineering degree (Smith College 2000).

There are similar examples at the precollege level. For example, research on single-sex Catholic schools found that per-pupil expenditures at boys' schools were 25 percent higher than those at girls' schools, and 30 percent higher than those at coed schools (Riordan 1990, 63).

Money is an issue in other ways as well. All-girl classes in coed schools can be a "cheap fix." Using existing teachers and resources incurs little if any costs but shows that schools and administrators are doing something about the "girl problem" in math and the sciences. Money can also be a motivation, as it was in the California public school single-sex experiment mentioned above, where the districts that applied were motivated by the money rather than a belief in the value of single-sex education (Datnow, Hubbard, and Woody 2001). As in so many other areas, money is an issue in single-sex schooling.

Assumption #5

Nothing can be done to stop boys from disrespecting girls and creating a difficult environment, so girls are safer and more comfortable in single-sex schools.

Studies have found that boys are more apt to cause classroom disruptions than girls, and also that boys receive both more negative and more positive attention in classrooms (Bailey et al. 1992). Indeed, one study found that teachers were surprised at the extent to which the dominant and harassing behavior of boys was impeding girls' educational progress (Parker and Rennie 1996). However, it has also been found that girls were not the only ones whose education was negatively affected. The same study found that while girls in single-sex classes received the least harassment from other students, boys in single-sex classes received the most (Parker and Rennie 1996).

Moreover, sexism occurs in all forms of schooling—single-sex female, single-sex male, and coed. While the quantity of sexist incidents (comments and behaviors) across different types of schools was the same, the types were different. In the single-sex female schools, sexist incidents were more apt to be in the form of allowing and/or reinforcing gender stereotypes by encouraging dependent behavior by girls and by less-than-rigorous instruction. Sexist incidents of explicit sexuality, defined as "the treatment of males or females as sexual objects," were found only in all-boys' schools. And the most prevalent form of sexism in coed schools was boys' domination of girls (Lee, Marks, and Byrd 1994, 103–4).

As a number of reports have noted, including AAUW's 1993 *Hostile Hallways* and its 2001 update, the hallways and classrooms of many of our schools are hostile to girls *and* to boys. The obvious difficulty with sex segregation as a solution to this hostility is that the *real* problems are simply avoided. A teacher who permits a student to ridicule another student on the basis of sex or any other characteristic is not only actively preventing the second student from learning but also intimidates other students. Many of the problems we attribute to students are actually teachers' failures to control the learning environment in their classrooms.

By removing the girls rather than dealing with the issues of classroom misbehavior and disrespect that are creating the problem in the first place, we are assuming a stereotyped view of girls as gentle, weak creatures who can't handle the rough environment of the real world. Moreover, we are implicitly accepting these beliefs:

- Boys' behavior is naturally incorrigible.
- The acceptable standard of classroom behavior is set by the most aggressive boys.

- It is acceptable for aggressive boys to prey on weaker boys and disrupt their learning.
- The appropriate female response to male aggression is not to fight back or to go to an authority but to leave, that appropriate "girl behavior" is to be passive.

Assumption #6

Sexual tension between girls and boys and the desire to impress each other is a distraction to learning that can be eliminated by single-sex schooling.

Separating girls and boys is seen as a way of reducing sexual distraction. However, for homosexual and bisexual youth, single-sex education hardly eliminates sexual tensions for them. The assumption that it does denies the existence of these youth and ignores their stresses. Moreover, aggressions in all-boys' schools are particularly an issue for boys who do not fit the ideal masculine stereotype (Datnow, Hubbard, and Woody 2001).

It is true that in many coed middle-school and high-school classes, students and teachers report that girls distract boys and boys distract girls. It is felt that girls are discouraged from speaking up and taking initiative because they are concerned about appearing either stupid to the boys, or on the contrary, too smart. Boys are felt to act up more than they otherwise would in order to impress girls (Durost 1996; Parker and Rennie 1996). We cannot assume that all classroom tensions and distractions are sexual. Girls want to impress each other too, and the same goes for boys. And everyone wants to impress the most popular students. Gangs, cliques, even clothing all create distractions. Indeed, student uniforms are also touted as a way of decreasing distractions.

As indicated earlier, the obvious difficulty with sex segregation as a solution to classroom climate issues, whether they are student misbehavior or student distractions, is that the *real* problems are behavioral and controllable. As adults and as educators, it is our responsibility to create a school climate that is safe and appropriate for girls and boys, gays, lesbians, bisexuals and straights, African Americans, Asian Americans, Hispanics, Native Americans, and whites. "School is a place where everyone can learn" must be more than a slogan.

One reason for teachers' failure to ensure respect in the classroom is the failure of the teacher education establishment and the education profession as a whole to emphasize the role of gender in learning (Sanders 1997; Sanders and Campbell 2001). Teachers who do not understand gender issues are ill prepared to deal with those issues in their classes.

Assumption #7

The existence of single-sex schooling for girls for the few does no harm to coed education for the many.

A major reason for the existence of girls' schools is in response to the well-documented failures of coeducation to provide an equitable learning environment (Bailey et al. 1992). An unintended result of single-sex schooling as a solution to girls' education dilemmas can be to serve as a pressure valve to release coeducation to deal with gender issues in education. Parents who are concerned enough about the quality of education their daughters are receiving to place them in girls' schools are no longer available to exert equity pressure on their neighborhood coed public schools. In the best of educational situations, parents are actively involved in their children's educations, but only in those schools their children attend. When they take their daughters out of the neighborhood school, that school loses access to the parents' voice and influence on the issue that concerns them so greatly: the education of girls. In the same way, coed public schools that choose to set up single-sex math or science classes, and the number of such schools that have done and are doing this is not negligible, are essentially removing any incentive for their normal math and science classes to change.

Assumption #8

Single-sex schooling provides girls with the best education.

Before we can even begin to determine if single-sex schooling has the potential to provide girls with the best education, we must first attempt to answer these questions:

- What is a good education?
- Does a good education differ for girls and boys?
- Do *all* girls and all boys need different things to get a good education?
- Does a good education differ if it is within a single-sex male, single-sex female, or coeducational environment?

We as educators and feminists have thought long and hard about these questions and have our own answers. Our goals for education center around the ability of students, both female and male, to develop the skills and capacity to control their own lives and to develop compassion and concern for others, along with the skills and capacity to take action on that compassion and concern. We believe that individuals need different things in order to receive that good education, but to define what students need based on group membership rather than individual characteristics is inappropriate as well as inaccurate.

We also believe that these questions must be answered individually and collectively by educators and others. Unless it is clear what a good education is, it makes little sense to design and implement strategies to move us toward a good education. It is clear to us that few definitions of good education would be achieved by simply separating girls and boys.

IN CLOSING

It is a disservice to frame the current discussion about the efficacy of single-sex education and coeducation as an either-or debate, with individuals on one side or the other. The debate needs to be reshaped into a thoughtful conversation, with an acknowledgment that our shared goal is schooling that fully educates *each* girl and *each* boy. That job is far from done, and that is where we need to dedicate our efforts (Campbell and Wahl 1998a).

Following is a parable about babies in the river: *Once upon a time there were three people walking next to the Hudson River. Looking over, they saw the river was full of babies. One of the three jumped into the river and started throwing babies out to the shore; the second jumped into the river and started teaching the babies to swim while the third started running upstream. "What are you doing?" cried the two in the water to the third. "There are babies drowning in the river!" "I know," said the third, "I'm going to find out who's throwing babies into the river and make them stop"* (Campbell and Hoey 1999).

To save all the babies we need to focus on what is needed to make the coeducational classroom fully equitable, promoting excellent outcomes for both girls and boys, in environments of high expectations. Well-funded, small-scale efforts in single-sex or coed schools will help save some babies, one by one, and even teach a few to swim. But without our best efforts directed toward *all* forms of education—coed, single sex, private, public, homeschooling—the babies will keep coming down the river. We should be able to do better than this.

NOTES

1. A chapter in *Doing Gender in Policy and Practice: Perspectives on Single Sex and Coeducational Schooling*, ed. Amanda Datnow and Lea Hubbard (New York: Routledge Falmer, 2002), 31–46.

2. Since there are so few single-sex male colleges and universities, Astin (1993) included institutions whose enrollment was 90 percent or more male as predominantly male.

3. The United States General Accounting Office (1996, pp. 6–7) concluded in a report to the U.S. House of Representatives that restricting enrollment in a public school by sex violated Title IX of the Education Amendments of 1972, and may also violate the equal protection clauses of the U.S. Constitution and different state constitutions.

4. It should be noted that there is a similar range in the political beliefs of those who support coeducation. Some support coeducation because boys benefit from the purported "civilizing influence" that girls bring to the classroom but still receive the larger share of resources and attention (Gill 1996, 3). Others see coeducation as offering the best hope for reframing schooling so that it is not determined by gender (Gill 1996, 5) while still others are concerned that prolonged exposure to single-sex education can lead to a "deficit approach" to girls' education, implying that girls are lacking in some ways compared to boys (Campbell and Wahl 1998a).

5. If we are to understand girls and boys, we must look at the complexities of who they are, which includes their sex but is not limited to it. Race/ethnicity, poverty level, and disability are just three of the demographic characteristics that interact with a child's sex to influence their lives.

6. Darrell Huff's 1954 *How to Lie with Statistics* (New York: W. W. Norton) provides an informative and entertaining overview of the problems with using "average" differences.

7. This argument is adapted from Patricia B. Campbell and Lesli Hoey, *Saving Babies and the Future of SMET in America* (Washington, DC: United States Congress Commission on the Advancement of Women and Minorities in Science, Engineering, and Technology Development (CAWMSET), 1999.

8. Campbell and Hoey, *Saving Babies.*

REFERENCES

American Association of University Women Educational Foundation. 1993. *Hostile hallways: AAUW's survey on sexual harassment in America's schools.* Washington, DC.

American College Testing. 1998. *Are America's students taking more science and mathematics course work?* ACT Research Report Series 98.2 [online]. At www.act.org/research/briefs/98-2.html.

Astin, Alexander. 1993. *What matters in college: Four critical years revisited.* San Francisco: Jossey-Bass.

Bailey, Susan, Lynn Burbidge, Patricia B. Campbell, Barbara Jackson, Fern Marx, and Peggy McIntosh. 1992. *The AAUW report: How schools shortchange girls.* Washington, DC: AAUW Educational Foundation and National Education Association.

Bennett, Susan M. 1997. California's single-gender academies pilot program. Paper presented at the National Dropout Prevention Conference, New Orleans.

Brody, Celeste, et al. 2000. *Gender consciousness and privilege.* New York: Falmer Press.

Campbell, Patricia B. 1995. A comparison of the Citadel and VMI to Converse College and Mary Baldwin. Unpublished manuscript.

Campbell, Patricia B., and Lesli Hoey. 1999. *Saving babies and the future of SMET in America.* Washington, DC: United States Congress Commission on the Advancement of Women and Minorities in Science, Engineering, and Technology Development (CAWMSET).

Campbell, Patricia B., and Ellen Wahl. 1998a. Of two minds: Single-sex education, coeducation, and the search for gender equity in K–12 public schooling. *New York Law School Journal of Human Rights* 14, part 1: 289–310.

——. 1998b. What's sex got to do with it?: Simplistic questions, complex answers. In *Separated by sex: A critical look at single-sex education for girls,* 63–74. Washington, DC: AAUW Educational Foundation.

Catsambis, Sophia. 1995. Gender, race, ethnicity, and science education in the middle grades. *Journal of Research in Science Teaching* 32 (3): 243–57.

Crosby, F., B. Allen, T. Culbertson, C. Wally, J. Morith, R. Hall, and B. Nunes. 1994. Taking selectivity into account, how much does gender composition matter?: A reanalysis of M. E. Tidball's research. *NWSA Journal* 6:107–18.

Datnow, Amanda, Lea Hubbard, and Elisabeth Woody. 2001. *Is single-gender schooling viable in the public sector? Lessons from California's pilot program.* Toronto: Ontario Institute for Studies in Education.

Durost, Richard A. 1996. Single-sex math classes: What and for whom? One school's experiences. *NASSP Bulletin* (February): 27–31.

Dwyer, Carole, and Linda M. Johnson. 1997. Grades, accomplishments and correlates. In *Gender and fair assessment*, ed. Warren Willingham and Nancy Cole. Englewood, NJ: Lawrence Erlbaum Press.

Educational Testing Service. 1997. ETS study finds more gender similarities than differences in educational performance. Princeton, NJ: Educational Testing Service. May 6.

Gill, Judith. 1996. Different contexts: similar outcomes. Paper presented at the annual meeting of the American Educational Research Association, New York.

Gilson, Judith E. 1999. Single-gender education versus coeducation for girls: A study of mathematics achievement and attitudes toward mathematics of middle-school students. Paper presented at the annual meeting of the American Educational Research Association, Montreal.

Haag, Pamela. 1998. Single-sex education in grades K–12. What does the research tell us? In *Separated by sex: A critical look at single-sex education for girls*. Washington, DC: AAUW Educational Foundation.

Hall, Roberta M., and Bernice R. Sandler. 1982. *The classroom climate: A chilly one for women?* Washington, DC: Association of American Colleges.

Hollinger, Debra K. 1993. *Single-sex schooling: Perspectives from practice and research: Volumes I & II. Special report.* Washington, DC: Office of Educational Research and Improvement, U.S. Department of Education.

Hyde, Janet S., Elizabeth Fennema, and Susan J. Lamon. 1990. Gender differences in mathematics performance: A meta-analysis. *Psychological Bulletin* 107 (2): 139–55.

Hyde, Janet S., and Marcia Linn. 1988. Gender differences in verbal ability: A meta-analysis. *Psychological Bulletin* 104:53–69.

Leder, Gilah, and Helen Forgasz. 1994. Single-sex mathematics classes in a coeducational setting. Paper presented at the annual meeting of the American Educational Research Association, Chicago.

Lee, Valerie. 1998. Is single-sex schooling a solution to the problem of gender inequity? In *Separated by sex: A critical look at single-sex education for girls*, 41–52. Washington, DC: AAUW Educational Foundation.

Lee, Valerie E., and Anthony S. Bryk. 1986. Effects of single-sex secondary schools on student achievement and attitudes. *Journal of Educational Psychology* 78 (5): 381–95.

——. 1989. Effects of single-sex schools: Response to Marsh. *Journal of Educational Psychology* 81 (4): 647–50.

Lee, Valerie E., and Helen M. Marks. 1990. Sustained effects of the single-sex secondary school experience on attitudes, behaviors, and values in college. *Journal of Educational Psychology* 82 (3): 578–92.

——. 1992. Who goes where? Choice of single-sex and coeducational independent secondary schools. *Sociology of Education* 65: 226–53.

Lee, Valerie E., Helen M. Marks, and Tina Byrd. 1994. Sexism in single-sex and coeducational independent secondary school classrooms. *Sociology of Education* 67: 92–120.

LePore, Paul C., and Robert Warren. 1996. The advantages of single-sex Catholic secondary schooling: Selection effects, school effects, or "much ado about nothing?" Paper presented at the annual meeting of the American Educational Research Association, New York.

Levit, Nancy. 1999. Separating equals: Educational research and the long-term consequences of sex segregation. *George Washington Law Review* 67 (3): 451–526.

Maccoby, Eleanor E., and Carol Jacklin. 1974. The psychology of sex differences. Stanford, CA: Stanford University Press.

National Center for Education Statistics. 2000. *The digest of education statistics 1999.* Washington, DC: U.S. Department of Education, NCES 2000-031.

National Coalition of Girls' Schools. 1998. Parents, students opting for all-girl education: Rising enrollment shows girls' schools in renaissance. November. At www.ncgs.org/Pages/news.htm#.

——. 2000. Girls' schools alumnae research: Executive summary. Concord, MA.

National Science Foundation. 1999. *Women, minorities and people with disabilities in science and engineering 1998.* Arlington, VA: Author (NSF 99-97).

——. 2000. *Women, minorities and people with disabilities in science and engineering 2000.* Arlington, VA: Author (NSF 00-327).

Nicholson, Heather Johnson. 1992. Gender issues in youth development programs. Washington, DC: Carnegie Council on Adolescent Development.

Parker, Leslie. 1985. *A strategy for optimizing the success of girls in mathematics: Report of a project of national significance.* Canberra, Australia: Commonwealth Schools Commission.

Parker, Leslie, and Leonie Rennie. 1996. Single-sex grouping: Issues for school administrators. Paper presented at the American Educational Research Association annual meeting, New York.

Pipher, Susan. 1994. *Reviving Ophelia: Saving the selves of adolescent girls.* New York: Grosset/Putnam.

Riordan, Cornelius. 1990. *Girls and boys in school: Together or separate?* New York: Teachers College Press.

——. 1992. Single and mixed gender colleges for women: Educational attitudes and occupational outcomes. *Review of Higher Education* 327: 336–45.

——. 1998. The future of single-sex schools. In *Separated by sex: A critical look at single-sex education for girls*, 53–62. Washington, DC: AAUW Educational Foundation.

Sadker, Myra, and David Sadker. 1994. *Failing at fairness: How our schools cheat girls.* New York: Touchstone.

Sanders, Jo. 1997. Teacher education and gender equity. *ERIC Digest* 96 (3).

Sanders, Jo, and Patricia B. Campbell. 2001. Making it happen: The role of teacher education in ensuring gender equity. In *Policy Perspectives: Expanding Public Policy Issues in Teacher Education*, ed. Dan Laitsch, vol. 2, no. 4, 1–5. American Association of Colleges for Teacher Education. May.

Sax, Linda. 1994. Challenging tokenism: The impact of major sex-composition on college student achievement. Paper presented at the annual meeting of the American Educational Research Association, New Orleans.

Smith College. 2000. News from Smith College. At www.smith.edu/newsoffice/Releases/00-094.html.

Smith, S. 1986. *Separate tables? An investigation into single-sex settings in mathematics.* London: Her Majesty's Stationery Office.

Thom, Mary. 2001. *Balancing the equation: Where are the girls in science, engineering and technology.* New York: National Council on Research on Women.

Tidball, M. Elizabeth, and Vera Kistiakowsky. 1976. Baccalaureate origins of American scientists and scholars. *Science*: 646, 648, 652.

United States General Accounting Office. 1996. *Public education issues involving single-gender schools and programs: A report to the Chairman, Committee on the Budget.* House of Representatives GAO/HEHS, 96–122. Washington DC: General Accounting Office.

United States v. Virginia et al. Nos. 94-1941 and 94-2107, 1997.

Wenglinsky, Harold. 2000. *How teaching matters; bringing the classroom back into discussions of teacher quality.* Princeton, NJ: Educational Testing Service.

Willingham, Warren, and Nancy Cole. 1997. *Gender and fair assessment.* Englewood, NJ: Lawrence Erlbaum Press.

Wood, Bonnie S., and Lorrie A. Brown. 1997. Participation in an all-female Algebra I class: Effects on high school math and science course selection. *Journal of Women and Minorities in Science and Engineering* 3 (4): 265–78.

AND THE WALLS COME TUMBLING DOWN

Lifting the Barriers—Six Hundred Tested Strategies that Really Work to Increase Girls' Participation in Science, Mathematics, and Computers

Jo Sanders, Director, Center for Gender Equity,
Washington Research Institute, Seattle, Washington

Jo Sanders published this work in 1994. Nevertheless, except in rare instances, what was true and applicable in the 1990s remains true and applicable now. The only things that may make this work appear dated would be occasional mentions to the '90s as current, and references to software and technologies that have since been replaced by newer ones.

EVERY STRATEGY IN THIS BOOK WAS CREATED AND CARRIED OUT BY A K–12 EDUCATOR

In 1990 to 1993, two hundred educators—primarily classroom teachers of computers, mathematics, and science, with a number of building and district administrators—participated in the Computer Equity Expert Project, which I directed. The two hundred represented every state in the United States. About half were involved with computer instruction, with the remainder fairly evenly split between science and math.

They applied because girls in their schools were turning down opportunities that were available to them in math, science, and computers. Girls tended not to enroll in advanced courses. They tended not to be involved in extracurricular activities. The educators weren't sure why, nor did they know what to do about it, but they were concerned.

After a weeklong seminar on gender equity in computers, math, and science, the two hundred educators returned to their schools and taught two workshops to their colleagues, each two and a half hours long: *What Is Computer Equity and Computer Equity in Math and Science* by myself and Mary McGinnis. The educators, whom we now called trainers, formed "equity teams" consisting of a few classroom teachers and administrators, and in some cases girls, parents, and/or school board members as well, to decide upon and carry out strategies to reverse girls' avoidance of science, math, and computers. In some cases, trainers did not have the benefit of equity teams and acted on their own.

Although they had received many ideas of strategies in materials and sessions at their seminary, my staff and I soon discovered that trainers and their colleagues wanted to develop their *own* strategies. Sometimes these were compelling local variations on themes we had provided them; other times their strategies were of breathtaking originality.

The results of their strategies were frankly stunning. Here is a small but representative sample of what they achieved in their schools within the space of a year or less.

Maine: For the first time in twelve years, girls signed up for physics.

New York: The ratio of girls to boys in the computer lab after school used to be 2:25. Now it is 1:1.

Wyoming: Girls' enrollment in physics rose from 56 percent to 62 percent, and in Introduction to Calculus, from 45 percent to 71 percent.

Oklahoma: In 1991, the elective computer science class had no girls. In 1992, it was 31 percent.

Nebraska: Precalculus enrollment, which had been 20 percent female, is now 45 percent female.

West Virginia: The computer club used to be 5 percent girls. Now it's 53 percent girls.

Montana: Programming class was 0 percent girls in 1990. In 1991 it was 14 percent. In 1992 it was 31 percent.

Massachusetts: The science club is now 80 percent female for the first time ever. Female enrollment in the upper-level math course increased 20 percent. The math team is now 50 percent female from less than 20 percent.

Colorado: 1991: 16 percent girls in Computer Programming. In 1992: 30 percent.

Arizona: Enrollment in upper-level math and science courses is up from 18 percent in 1991 to 30 percent in 1992.

Virginia: The Advanced Placement Pascal class went from 0 percent to 50 percent girls in a year.

Mississippi: In 1991 the high school's academic team in math and science competitions was composed of seven boys and two girls. This year, it is composed of seven girls and two boys.

Oregon: Girls' enrollment in Advanced Math rose from 37 percent to 64 percent over the last year. For Advanced Chemistry, it was 20 percent to 63 percent.

District of Columbia: Girls' free-time use of computers doubled during the project.

We learned about what was happening in trainers' schools in lengthy telephone interviews and other contacts, and soon realized that collectively these two hundred people were a treasure chest of creativity and solutions to a nationwide, indeed worldwide, problem. I am delighted to be able to share with you the fruits of their efforts.

I invite you to browse through the strategies. Adopt or adapt those that you like, or use them as springboards for your own ideas. As you will soon see, strategies range from the simple to the complex. Most, however, are just about effortless, and while a few cost something, the majority cost nothing at all. *Note: These strategies are highly transferable*!

- Many computer strategies are also useful in science and math environments, and vice versa. Don't eliminate a strategy from consideration merely because the trainer who invented it used it in a subject you don't teach.
- Many strategies used with high-school girls are also useful with younger girls, and vice versa.
- Many strategies used with girls are also useful with boys in underrepresented subjects, children of color, at-risk children, and children with disabilities.

THE PRINCIPLES OF GENDER EQUITY

Although this book contains more than six hundred strategies, the principles underlying them are far fewer.

Focus specifically on girls. Since the problem is that girls think that math, science, and computers are not appropriate for girls, you have to make it clear to them that this isn't true. It isn't enough to tell girls that advanced courses or extracurricular activities are available for *all* students, or for *girls and boys*: their preconceptions prevent them from believing it. Being evenhanded won't do it. There is no alternative to carrying out strategies that say *girls*, loud and clear.

Design activities around girls' interests. It has been the case that much curriculum in mathematics, science, and computers was based on typical male interests, since the primary "consumers" of mathematics, science, and computer education were thought to be males. The physics of rocketry, for example, might not fall within many girls' experience. Expand your curriculum. Figure out what girls are interested in, or just ask them, and incorporate those interests in your lessons. (However, see "The Equity Trap.")

Emphasize usefulness. Many girls seem to relate to a school subject in terms of how useful it is now or will be to them in the future, while many boys seem comfortable exploring a subject for its own sake. Each approach has its own advantages and disadvantages, but in the meantime it is helpful to carry out strategies that relate your subject to real-world connections, impacts, and uses.

Highlight the social aspect. Adolescent girls especially have a strong need for social contact. They seem to go from class to class in packs, not individually. Make the herd instinct and peer pressure work *for* you for a change by carrying out strategies that involve girls in groups, not individually.

Watch your language. Sex stereotypes are mostly conveyed through subtle, unintentional means. A good example is language. When mathematicians, scientists, or computer specialists are always referred to as "he," girls eventually get the idea that "she" is not quite appropriate. In the same way, the Logo turtle is "it," not "he," and girls in math, science, and computer class are not "guys."

Eliminate biased practices. If you find yourself assigning responsibilities and tasks to boys, or if the volunteers you get for them are boys, or if the scheduling of a currently male-intensive activity makes it hard for girls to attend, or if you let students choose the equipment they will use and the boys get to the best equipment first, or if you call on boys more than girls, it's time to think about and to correct inadvertently biased practices.

Spread the word. It is surprising how many people are generally unaware of sex stereotypes and gender bias, such as the lone woman in a large math, science, or computer department who hasn't thought about the gender implications of the fact that all her peers are men. Your colleagues as well as your students need to learn how to recognize gender bias, why it matters, and how to correct it. The shared responsibility is easier on you as well.

Do it all again next year. No matter what strategies you carry out this year and what success you have, most girls coming into your class or your school next year will not have heard the equity message yet. Eventually gender equity becomes part of the school climate, so that girls who are new to the school will assume that this is what "the big kids" have always done. You needn't tell them otherwise.

Once you assimilate these few principles, you will understand why almost any strategy that expresses them will work. I am quite sure that should you choose to, you will be able to generate many strategies not included here.

A FEW MORE OBSERVATIONS

All this having been said, there are a few more important points that deserve some attention.

Men Are Not the Problem; Women Are Not the Solution

People who don't understand the dynamics of gender inequity often assume that girls are underrepresented in science, mathematics, and technology because men are keeping them out. All would be well, this thinking goes, if only *women* were the teachers, administrators, etc.

The simplicity is tempting, but the theory is false. Years of everyday experience as well as research have convinced me that men can be as supportive of girls' achievement in computers, math, and science as women, and that women can be as sexist as men. You simply can't predict by sex alone which people will be supportive of a gender equity effort and which ones won't. (By the way, by "sex" I mean what you're born with. "Gender" refers to what you learn.)

The reason is that we all of us, certainly including me, learned our sexism from the same place: the society at large. Starting with pink and blue receiving blankets and progressing on through toys, television, movies, and books, and especially by observing other people, we all learned that some forms of behavior and belief are more appropriate for one sex or the other. Parents—mothers as well as fathers, other relatives, friends, neighbors, teachers, and public figures all passed on a gender-biased legacy to us without intending to. Their childhoods were gender biased because their parents' were, and on back through the generations. You can only teach, consciously or unconsciously, what you know yourself. Most of these lessons are so basic that we don't realize we learned them, but the proof is in the discomfort many of us feel at the prospect of crossing a sex-role boundary line.

This is why it is not only wrong to blame men for sexism—women can be just as sexist—but pointless. After all, men have daughters they care about. Sexism is rarely deliberate. Instead, it's usually the unintended result of thoughtlessness, inattention, and mistaken assumptions.

It's far more constructive for all of us, men and women alike, to make an effort to understand the dynamics of sexism. It really is not necessary in the 1990s for girls to decline opportunities in math, science, and computers just because these fields have for decades been traditionally associated with males. Girls' own futures and the challenges of the twenty-first century necessitate a revised notion of who should and shouldn't do math, science, and computers. So let's drop the blaming and get to it.

Single-Sex versus Coed

There has been a great deal of controversy over single-sex versus coed learning environments for children.

First, you need to know that single-sex learning environments are legal under Title IX only on the condition that they are established to counteract the effects of previous sex discrimination. In other words, if girls have been excluded, officially or unofficially, from educational opportunities in the past—such as advanced courses or extracurricular programs that were primarily or entirely male—then it is legal to establish a single-sex version of the course or program as a remedial measure.

Second, you need to know that single-sex learning environments work extremely well. Many girls prefer them and learn better and faster in them. Research has established this repeatedly and conclusively.

I am nevertheless uncomfortable with single-sex environments. Just as I would find it morally repugnant to segregate white children and children of color even for purposes of improved education for the children of color, so I find sex-segregated education undesirable. If the problem is that boys' behavior makes it difficult for girls to learn well, the solution is to improve the boys' behavior, not segregate the girls in some kind of protective cocoon. We can't keep girls there forever, so we may as well deal now with the problems that make a cocoon tempting.

The real world is rarely so unambiguous, though. Many of the trainers created single-sex learning environments in classes and especially in extracurricular events simply because the approach is so very effective. You may choose to do so as well. If you do, I would urge you to keep up the segregated approach only until girls' interests in math, science, or technology are firmly established, at which point you should be able to move on to a coed environment. After all, how long will you want to run a dual system?

The Equity Trap

There is no doubt that strategies which connect computers, science, and mathematics to girls' existing interests work well. For example, since many girls are interested in the human body, it makes sense to tie some computer, science, and math lessons and extracurricular activities to the human body.

This perfectly obvious approach has a built-in problem, however. In a society where sexist legacies are inevitable, many girls learn early on to have sex-stereotyped interests. They learn to be interested in dolls, not trucks; makeup, not football; people, not things; and writing, not science. So by appealing to girls' existing interests, you are unintentionally reinforcing the status quo in sex-role stereotypes. (My favorite metaphor for this is getting girls interested in computers by having them use a cosmetics simulation program!) On the other hand, if you try to appeal to an interest many girls do not currently have in order to broaden their horizons, they are not likely to respond because they're not interested.

This is the equity trap, and it's rather serious. If we content ourselves with following girls' existing interests, we not only reinforce sex-role stereotypes but we also lose the many advantages to boys' interests.

It has often been noted, for example, that many girls use computers for a specific purpose, to get homework or a project done. Many boys prefer to "mess around" with a computer, playing games or just to see what it can do. Compared to how girls use computers, boys waste a lot of time, but on the other hand, boys' approach is likelier to achieve real mastery, confidence, and control over the medium. Similarly, it has often been noted that many girls have learned to follow direction, procedures, or rules in solving a math problem. This saves time and often leads to the right answer, but not following directions—inventing your own way along a problem—often has the benefit of teaching you far more than you could otherwise learn. (The reverse is also true. There is a great deal to be said for boys becoming more efficient, wasting less time, and getting more right answers, to say nothing of sharing more of the human condition: caring for small children, running a household, and maintaining loving friendships.)

The only solution I know to the equity trap is the incremental one of stretching girls' interests a little at a time. Mentioning unfamiliar topics often and in varied ways, and relating unfamiliar topics to familiar ones, will eventually make them familiar and interesting. Using role models to stretch girls' horizons is another method.

Just be aware of the equity trap as you plan your strategies. Try not to appeal to girls' sex-stereotyped interests just because they work, but rather keep your eye on their adult futures, when it will serve them much better to have a full range of traditionally masculine as well as feminine interests, skills, talents, and abilities.

Equity for Girls Is Equity for Everyone

In many years of conducting projects in schools dealing with gender equity in computers, math, and science for girls, I have learned that the projects always lead to improved education for boys as well. For me, this outcome is not exactly unintended.

It happens because the process of focusing on girls' educational needs—figuring out what the barriers are, what's going wrong, and what should be improved, and offering teachers better materials and ways of teaching—inevitably yields benefits that result in better educations for boys as well. For example, you can't learn that you have been calling mostly on boys in class and not use the knowledge to pay more attention not only to girls but also to unassertive, quiet boys. You can't learn how to call on girls more often without teaching dominant boys that they cannot have more than their fair share of your attention. You can't learn better curriculum for girls without learning better curriculum for boys.

And beyond these advantages, it is certainly good for boys in school to learn that their female classmates are equal in competence, intelligence, and ambition, and that women have achieved and are achieving much in the work of the world.

So if you're uncomfortable about "special treatment" for girls in these strategies, don't be. The strategies will make you a better educator for everyone.

CONTESTS AND COMPETITIONS

Following are various types of contents and competitions:

- Encourage girls to apply for programs in which they work with mathematicians or scientists over the summer and receive a stipend.
- If your school doesn't participate in competitive activities such as Computer Learning Month, have girls gather signatures on a petition to reverse the policy.
- Hold a "Where in the World is Carmen Sandiego?" contest. Invite girls to the computer room at lunchtime over a two-week period to compete on the game.
- Urge girls to enter MathCounts competitions in teams. Encourage parents to support them.
- Encourage a team of girls to enter the Erector Set Contest, which involves designing and building a structure.
- Through your state professional association, start a statewide contest open not to individuals but to teams composed of three girls and three boys.
- Hold a school contest for the best program using low-resolution graphics and animation. Encourage girls to enter.
- Tell students you will take students with the best class projects to visit a nearby university's Women in Engineering Program.
- Create an all-girl programming team for the countywide competition.

And here are other types of competition strategies:

- Have girls design problems and judge solutions for an academic contest.
- Talk talented female students into entering competitions in pairs or small groups.
- Encourage girls to enter essay contests and write about scientific, mathematical, or technical topics.
- Urge school board members and district administrators not to permit any math, science, or technology competitive team consisting only of boys.

COUNSELORS

These strategies are appropriate for teachers and administrators as well as counselors.

Course and Career Advising

- Urge girls to take advanced courses in math, science, or technology.
- Do not permit girls to drop math, science, or technology courses without discussing with them how important these subjects are for their future.
- Hold a discussion with girls on how they feel they are treated in math, science, or computer class. They may be more willing to speak to a counselor rather than their teachers since their grades are not at risk.
- When you see that a female student has not signed up for an advanced course you think she should be taking, do some one-on-one counseling with her.
- Go to your feeder schools and meet with counselors there. Describe why you need their help in encouraging girls to sign up for math, science, or technology courses.
- Don't wait for a girl to express an interest in an advanced course: suggest it to her first.

- Forge better links with counselors at the vocational-technical school your district's students attend. Speak to them about the importance of enabling girls to succeed in technical fields.
- Obtain materials on nontraditional careers and discuss them with girls.
- Get administrators to require that counselors urge girls to take advanced courses and consider nontraditional careers.
- Meet with science, math, and computer teachers to learn more about what the classes involve and how to advise students better.
- Be alert for counselors who believe that an advanced course with many girls must be watered down. Try to correct the error and make sure it isn't passed on to students.
- Don't let girls drop a course because they "only got a B" in it.
- Urge high-school girls who are interested in math, science, or technology to consider attending a technical college rather than a liberal arts college.
- Tell girls not to listen to people who tell them what their limits are.
- Make posters about single-parent families and poverty levels in your area, and about how the more math you take the better your chances are for a well-paying job. Show these to girls and discuss fully.
- Ask to speak to girls in homeroom or at another time about the career opportunities that programming ability, math, or science opens to them.

Personal and Self-Esteem Issues

- Look a girl in the eye and tell her, "You're really good at this."
- Hold an after-school discussion group on women's rights, meeting monthly. Topics can include the depiction of women in music videos, sexist comments and incidents in school, and date rape.
- Hold assertiveness and self-defense training for girls to help them deal with sexual aggression from boys.
- Hold sexual-harassment training for boys at the same time to help them stop being sexually aggressive.
- After you hold a discussion with girls about how they feel they are treated in school, report on what they say to the faculty. If they don't believe you, videotape the girls' next discussion and show that.
- If boys make fun of girls in class to the point that girls feel reluctant to ask or answer questions, ask a teacher or another counselor to talk with the boys separately while you talk with the girls (or vice versa) about dealing with the problem.
- Hold a discussion group for girls who are much outnumbered by boys in technical classes to provide an outlet for feelings of pressure or discomfort they may have.
- Lead a discussion with girls on the pros and cons of (usually male) team sports.

CURRICULUM BY SUBJECT

Science

- Have students draw a picture of "a scientist." Discuss stereotyped features with particular attention to how they exclude women.
- Require that all science reports be word processed.
- If you need a lab assistant, choose a girl.
- Invite women scientists to speak to your students in class.
- Schedule all-girl labs to keep girls from sitting back while boys complete the work.
- Use a female mannequin.

- When a visual of a scientist is called for, show a female scientist.
- Have students read novels dealing with science to appeal to girls (and boys) who relate primarily to literature.
- Buy and use a science tool kit package with probes and sensors that can be used for measuring temperatures of living things and other uses.
- In science lab groups, require that girls not be the recorder. This gets them more actively involved in the lab work.
- Present information on science occupations and earnings annually to students.

Computers

- Pair girls at the computers, even if you have enough computers for everyone.
- Emphasize programming or desktop publishing rather than secretarial computer skills for high-school girls.
- Change the course description of a multimedia course from one that emphasizes the equipment to one that emphasizes the final products. Also refer to teamwork, cooperation, and fun.
- Do less programming and more hypertext authoring, multimedia, and/or robotics in computer class.
- As a term assignment in an advanced programming course, have students create an interactive game that has graphics, music, and a scorekeeping system, and offers positive feedback to the user. Students' games do not have to involve killing and destroying. They can focus on helping elementary students with practice in spelling, identifying female athletes and historical figures, simulation games with female detectives, and identifying '60s music correctly (with digitized music selections downloaded from a bulletin board). Use the games with younger students next year.
- Offer a girls-only Introduction to Computer Science class.
- Use popular singers in addition to or instead of using baseball statistics for a database lesson.
- Invite women computer specialists to speak to your students in class.
- Teach Logo, which tends to appeal more to girls, rather than BASIC. Refer to the Logo turtle as "it," not "he."
- Teach students how to do animation on a computer.
- Invite girls to be your computer aides. Ask them to be responsible for the technical cleanup at the end of the day: dumping files, etc.
- Get students involved in telecommunicating with students in other states or countries.
- Use Lego-Logo.
- Present information on technology occupations and earnings annually to students.

Math

- Invite a woman who owns a technical business to math class to talk about the math she uses in her business.
- Do a CD-ROM lesson on famous women in mathematics.
- Invite women mathematicians to speak to your students in class.
- Have students construct various types of graphs, manually or with a computer, illustrating labor market and earnings statistics.
- Add more manipulatives to the curriculum in the lower grades to boost girls' spatial skills.
- Use the Math Experimentation Toolkit for the computer.
- Present information on mathematics occupations and earnings annually to students.

Social Studies

- Include database activities.
- Obtain labor market statistics—how much people earn in technical and nontechnical occupations, and the proportion of women in each occupation—and teach it in social studies class. Discuss thoroughly. Follow it with related readings.
- For a class project, have a student research stereotypes of careers as appropriate for males or females and the realities of the labor market in terms of participation and earnings.

English/Language Arts

- As an English assignment, ask students to write a composition on this question: "How would your life be different if you woke up tomorrow the opposite sex?" (Variation: "a different race.")
- Start a written discussion on a computer about women's issues. Give students articles to read and ask them to write up their reactions and respond to each other's reactions.
- Assign more books to be read with women as protagonists, or do this as a special unit.
- Use desktop publishing software to produce stories that girls (and boys) write on a computer.
- Have students research a vocational field of their choice, write a paper, spend a day with a person in the field, and discuss their experiences with the class. Urge girls to select a technical field.

Geography

- A geography lesson can be on famous female American scientists and the states they are from.

Music

- Have students compose, orchestrate, and print music on a computer.

Physical Education or Health

- Do fitness graphs on every student on the computer.

Library

- Urge girls to use the online encyclopedia before the printed one.
- Have a special exhibit on women in literature.
- Use CD-ROM and other interactive video.
- Order books on women in various fields.

CURRICULUM BY GRADE

Kindergarten

- Read gender-equitable stories to children.
- Encourage girls to play with blocks as well as bridal veils.

Seniors

- Suggest that students do their senior project on an equity-related topic. Arrange for them to collect data in other school buildings if appropriate.
- Require that senior project reports be written on a computer.
- Integrate varied forms of technology into required senior projects.

All Grade Levels

- Include units on women achievers.
- If your school gives out rewards for good student behavior, let kids have extra time in the computer lab as a form of reward.
- Organize all-girl classes in math, science, and/or computers.
- Stress the usefulness of science, math, and computers to everyday situations, problems, and needs.
- During Women's History Month (or any time during the school year), present brief biographies of notable women in your field and ask students for the names of the achievers, or vice versa. Give small prizes to those who answer correctly.
- Increase the amount of hands-on computer use in classes.
- Assign a report on famous women in your subject. Have students ask the librarian for help if needed.
- Let other faculty know that girls are available to help them as computer experts and troubleshooters.
- Create an entire bulletin board on women in your field.
- Lead a class discussion on the pros and cons of having a special month devoted to women's achievements (Women's History Month in March).
- Use interesting software for remedial and review purposes.
- If there is no AP or advanced course in your subject, girls who want such a course can push for it with the administration.
- Ask girls to try out your new software. They can help you teach it to the other students.
- Hold frequent discussions about the career implications of your subject, and make sure girls are fully involved.
- Design curriculum units around interests you know many girls have.
- When girls are at the computer, make sure they are not doing only word processing.
- Read the district's policy on sexual harassment to all your students. Hold a discussion on it.

EXTRACURRICULAR CLUBS AND PROGRAMS

Types

These can be for girls only or you can recruit girls for coed groups. See the discussion of "Single Sex versus CoEd."

- Start a hands-on after-school club for girls.
- If existing clubs tend to be competitive, start a new one that isn't. It will appeal to most girls and a number of boys who aren't comfortable in a competitive atmosphere.
- Start a club limited to girls in one grade level.
- Start an after-school program for at-risk students, sponsored by the local Cooperative Extension Office or 4-H organization.
- Start a weekend program for a Brownies group and teach them hands-on science. Work with Girl Scouts after school in activities leading to merit badges in math, science, and computers.

- Start a Lunch Break with Telecommunications program.
- Start a summer math and science program or camp for third- through fifth-grade girls or for middle-school girls.
- Start a Math or Science League for Girls at lunchtime.
- Recruit girls actively for the video production team or the broadcast team.
- If you are running a successful program for elementary- or middle-school girls and they are graduating out of your school, get faculty members at their new school to continue your program there, or at least ask them to extend special invitations to the girls to continue their interests there.
- Sponsor a Girls' Computer Awareness Day to introduce them to telecommunications.
- Hold a career awareness fair that focuses on women in technology, math, and/or science.
- Arrange for your students to take part in a teleconference on women in math, science, or technology.
- Hold a panel discussion on careers in math, science, and engineering, with women panelists.
- On Math Awareness Day, have girls present probability and statistics.
- Identify summer programs in math, science, and/or computers in your area, especially those designed for girls. Send the information home with girls to parents.
- Hold a Computer Open House and make sure at least 50 percent of the tour guides and demonstrators are girls.
- Ask the local chapter of the American Association of University Women (AAUW) to help you put together a Career Day.
- Start a rocketry club for girls, or increase female participation in the existing all-male rocketry club.
- Hold a daylong program on science, math, and technology for "second-tier" girls, those who are the next level down from the highest achievers.
- Hold a special program in math, science, or computers for pregnant and parenting teenagers. Get grant money to pay for child care.
- Ask teachers to recommend girls who are peer leaders. Invite them once a week to a Lunch Bunch meeting in the computer lab, with any girlfriends who care to join them. Groom them to become teacher assistants and peer tutors.
- Hold a girls-only series of study sessions for remedial or enrichment purposes. As appropriate, use the computer.
- Work with your local YWCA to sponsor an after-school program for girls in math, science, and technology.
- Offer a one-month math and science summer camp for minority girls.
- Hold a Family Math program.
- Have your high school hold a Math Day for several elementary schools. Ask your female students to help you plan and run it. Have them play math games with the younger children.
- Give an assembly presentation to students on gender equity. Ask girls to participate as panelists.

Activities

Many of these ideas are also appropriate for classes.

Audiovisuals

- Show girls an old animated cartoon film, such as *Dudley Do-Right*, to show them the blatant level of sexism that was commonly accepted thirty years ago and to sensitize them to sexism in the '90s.
- At a holiday party, show a video about a girl deciding about a nontraditional career.

Awareness

- Periodically distribute handouts to students on the equity issue and its occupational ramifications. Ask them to take the handouts home to parents, too.
- Discussion topics for girls' equity groups: "Young Women and Advertising," "Teasing: Freedom of Speech or Something Else?"
- Have girls explore old school awards. If they find one using sexist language (such as a plaque awarded to the entire student body which reads "so that he [*sic*] may reach his full potential," they can write letters of protest to the school newspaper.
- Have a girl do a presentation on gender equity at the school's Student Senate.

Bulletin or Display Boards

- Have girls create a bulletin board on women in math, science, and/or technical careers, and display it in a well-traveled school hallway.
- Display girls' computer graphics work in the hallways.
- Have girls interview and photograph women in the community doing nontraditional jobs. Have them write captions and create display boards. Circulate the display boards to all schools in the district and show them as well at parent events.
- Make a timeline of the Renaissance period (or any other) and include as many women's achievements as possible in it. When it's completed, arrange for it to be exhibited in other district schools as well as your own.
- Start a computer "help wanted" bulletin board to connect students who need help with their computers or particular software with those who know the answers. Encourage girls to make good use of it both as helpers and "helpees."

Graphics

- Have girls make holiday cards on the computer.
- Have girls create a computer graphic about their computer club and transfer it to T-shirts.
- Teach girls how to use Pagemaker and make them responsible for at least some of the school's desktop publishing work.
- If your school has newly acquired computers, hold an introductory session for girls on graphics and other applications.
- For the school newspaper, have students do far more than word processing: picture art, clip art, graphics, use of a scanner, accessing encyclopedias and dictionaries via CD-ROM.
- Have girls make get-well cards on the computer for convalescents in a nearby hospital or nursing home.

Multimedia and Visual Presentations

- Have girls create a multimedia video scrapbook as an alternative or addition to the school yearbook. This can involve writing and filming skits, interviewing people on tape, editing, transferring to VHS, recording music and transferring that to tape as well, and others.
- Have girls create a tourism video about your town, using Hyperstudio Multimedia. Offer it to the Chamber of Commerce or the mayor's office.
- Teach girls how to use a CD-ROM.
- Create a multimedia *This Is Your Life* of a girl in the club. Show it at an open house for parents.
- Use Hypercard and a scanner to make slide shows and enhance student projects.

- Have students create a visual presentation on girls and boys in nontraditional roles, in slide-show, video-tape, or multimedia format. Show it to other students.
- Have kids create a multimedia project on women in politics.
- Have girls take photos or videos of club activities and use them in your professional presentations on gender equity.
- Have students create multimedia presentations on nontraditional careers.
- Create an electronic student portfolio to be maintained throughout the school years. Solicit advice on the project from girls (and boys).
- Use Hypercard with sound and graphics.

Software and Other Computer Activities

- Create a computer trivia game with questions on why many females avoid computers. Right-answer rewards and wrong-answer penalties can be as "feminine" or "macho" as you like.
- Arrange to let girls who prefer this use a smaller, more private computer room instead of the more public and conspicuous locations of other computers.
- Divide one large computer lab into three smaller ones reserved for girls, boys, and mixed.
- Have girls use a database of college scholarship information and write letters for more information using the computer.
- Place a computer with a modem in the library, and teach girls how to use it to access information electronically.
- Have girls teach word processing at lunchtime once a week to anyone who wants to learn. They can also make greeting cards using Print Shop or the equivalent for their friends.
- Have girls "own their own businesses" via computer: use spreadsheets to process income and expenses and project cash flow; use graphics programs to prepare advertising flyers and letterheads.
- Sign up for Prodigy to get girls interested in telecommunicating.
- Spend time on SAT preparation in the after-school computer club.
- To keep girls from using the same familiar software over and over, show them new software on a regular basis.
- If your school has an after-school chapter of Future Homemakers of America, get them to use a computer in their activities.
- Choose software that lets girls choose the name and sex of the main character.
- In a coed computer club, limit boys' use of war and conflict software.
- Lend out a laptop or notebook computer to girls (and boys) overnight and on weekends.
- When girls arrive in the computer lab without schoolwork to be done, show them interesting software.
- Introduce girls to CAD (computer-aided design) software.
- If you are the faculty adviser of groups such as the Student Council, encourage girls to use computers for administrative and publicity matters relating to the council.
- Have a girl introduce a new piece of software to the student body every week in the assembly time.
- In an election year, have girls write a computer program to tally votes in a mock presidential election. Hold the election in the school. Play Sousa marches.

Surveys

- Have girls survey their peers on science, math, or computer interests and activities. Have them present the results to the school board.
- Have girls conduct a career goal survey among students.

- Have girls complete a survey on their plans for working, child rearing, and combining the two. Compare their answers with national statistics indicating a majority of women with small children must work for economic reasons. Discuss the implications for their futures.
- Have girls conduct a survey on girls' favorite computer games. Try to get some for the school.
- Have girls design and conduct a survey of their peers on the gender issue and their expectations for the future, in part to ensure that you are assessing girls' attitudes and expectations correctly

Television

- Have girls write a script for a television public service announcement showing how girls are overlooked in the classroom and ways to avoid it. Try to get the announcement aired on TV.
- Have girls develop a skit about gender equity in math, science, or computers, perhaps about calling a computer repairman who turns out to be a computer repairwoman. Videotape the skit and show it to the school on the televised morning announcements.
- Arrange for a few girls and yourself to appear as panelists on a local-access television channel to discuss gender equity in education.

Writing

- Have girls put together a newsletter on equity developments for distribution to the entire faculty.
- Have girls write a newsletter about famous women, either locally or historically. Distribute it as widely as possible.
- Have girls write up the activities of their club for the school newspaper.
- Have a regular column on gender equity in the school newspaper, the PTA newsletter, and/or the district newsletter.
- Produce the school's literary magazine on a computer.
- Have girls compile a *Women in Our Community* pamphlet, and give it to libraries and bookstores.
- Let students use the computer as a message board.
- Girls can write letters of protest to companies whose products or advertisements they consider sexist.

Other Extracurricular Strategies

- Include attention to gender equity in math, science, and technology during Women's History Month.
- Organize a weekly Girls' Day in your club.
- Give girls bookmarks each time they come to the club: "Girls Can Do Computers," "Girls Can Fly Airplanes," etc. Eventually they will come for the club, not the bookmarks.
- Ask girls to decide how to use money raised from a local community organization for the club.
- Provide recycled computer parts from which girls can make jewelry.
- Ask girls to help out at the Science Fair.
- Hold an "affirmation session" where girls say such things as, "I'm great at math" and "I love computers" as loudly as they want.
- As part of a daylong special program, hold a banquet. Try to get food donated by local merchants.
- For a career fair, organize hands-on booths dealing with science, technology, and/or mathematics staffed by women or girls.
- When girls arrive in the computer or science lab who haven't been there for a while, make sure they know how to get started. When they leave, say, "Please come again." Make them feel welcome.

- Collect math and science games and puzzles to do in your club.
- Count the number of girls and boys who come to each extracurricular session, since glancing over the room to see who is there is often inaccurate. Keep track of the numbers over time.
- To increase girls' interest in a science club, let them know you'll be devoting some time to reproduction, embryology, dissection of an egg, and other topics of high female interest.
- Let girls decorate the science lab or computer room as they like, to make it feel more comfortable to be in.
- Open the lab at lunchtime for drop-in use. Encourage girls to make use of the equipment by doing little experiments: "fun labs."
- Build and construct things with girls, using skills and tools usually associated with boys.
- Keep calling to find out about dropouts from limited-enrollment community conferences or programs that you want girls to be involved in. When they occur, urge that more of your girls be accepted into the program.

FIELD TRIPS

Education Related

- Take girls to an Expanding Your Horizons conference in your area. This is a highly recommended strategy.
- Sign your school up to participate in a Women and Engineering program at your local college or university.
- Take girls to visit college math, science, and technology facilities and sit in on a class or two. Have faculty members or female students speak with them about scholarships and even postgraduation job placement help. Arrange for female college students to lead the tours. If you have too many girls to tour together, place friends in the same tour group.
- If your state has a residential science and math school for gifted students, take some girls on an overnight field trip. Meet with girls who go to the school. Attend a couple of classes. Speak with a couple of teachers. Stay overnight in the dorm if possible.

Employment Related

- Arrange visits to organizations such as research and educational centers, high-tech companies, an earthquake research center, a TV station, a hands-on science museum, a tour of a naval ship, a textile plant, etc., with tours conducted by female employees.
- Arrange a career-shadowing program with women scientists and engineers.
- Take girls to visit several ordinary offices to see the impact of technology on everyday work life.
- Take girls to the local airport to explore the use of computers in the aviation industry and learn about career opportunities.
- Have teachers nominate girls to participate in a tour of a superconducting computer center.

Other

- Take girls to a science museum.
- Send a female student to represent the school at a meeting on math and science for students.

- Take girls on an Outward Bound-type trip to build self-confidence.
- Take girls to a video parlor. Who do they see there? What do the games emphasize? What lessons can be drawn?
- During a class trip to Washington, D.C., visit the National Museum of Women in the Arts.

FUND-RAISING

Outside of School

- Ask your local AAUW chapter (American Association of University Women) to provide funds enabling you to take girls to special events.
- In exchange for a presentation on gender equity, ask a community group such as Delta Kappa Gamma to donate books to the school library on women's history.
- If you win an educational contest, donate your winnings to school with the preference that they be spent to enable girls to take advantage of community programs or courses.
- Raise money from a local women's club to buy Carmen Sandiego software and to pay cash prizes to contest winners.
- Obtain a Perkins (vocational education) grant for a program for girls ages fourteen to twenty-one on nontraditional careers for women. Use the money on videotapes about technical careers, guest speakers, field trips, and software.
- Ask local merchants to donate computer items—software, class fees, disks, etc.—as door prizes for a Computer Night for parents.

Among Students and Parents

- Charge students fifty cents per personalized greeting card, made by girls using Print Shop or the equivalent. Sell Santagrams, Heartograms, and so forth.
- Raise money for a field trip by having girls staff a car-wash service on a Saturday. (If you can't get out of it do a fashion show or bake sale, but try not to.)
- Sell to parents copies of a video yearbook tape that girls create and use the money to buy more electronic equipment or cameras.
- Charge a small fee for a mother-daughter computer event.
- Have a computer booth at the annual Halloween carnival, where kids pay ten cents for a Print Shop sign. Have the booth staffed by girls.
- Set up a program, which when students enter birthdates, prints out facts about that date. Format it like a certificate, print it out, tie it up with a ribbon, and present it like a gift. Charge a nominal fee.

MATERIALS

- Evaluate software, textbooks, and other curriculum materials for gender bias.
- Add books on women and gender equity to the school library.
- Choose gender-fair materials whenever possible. In those cases where older, inequitable materials must be used, discuss the sexism openly with students.
- Examine the posters and illustrations on the walls. If they show only or mostly men and boys, add women and girls.

- Examine the software you have for free-time use. If you discover a large amount of violent software, get rid of it (violent software isn't healthy for boys' psychosocial development either) or at least obtain a broader variety of software.
- Create your own posters of women in math and science by using photos of local women in these jobs.
- Get new software on a provisional basis. Be sure girls are interested in it before you buy it.
- Carry out periodic reviews of curriculum materials. Throw out texts that are biased if you can.
- If you find old sexist books in the school library, show them to girls as an example of how life used to be.

MENTORING

Girl-to-Girl Strategies

- Teach older girls how to help younger children in the computer lab.
- Have girls teach other girls how to use telecommunications.
- Have girls teach other girls how to use graphics software. Display creations in hallways and classrooms.
- Have fourth-grade girls "share stories" on the computer with kindergarten children.
- Take a group of middle-school girls to the elementary school to talk to the little girls about how important science, computers, and math are.
- Arrange for middle-school girls to "shadow" high-school girls and go with them to their advanced math and science classes.
- Select a few girls and a boy or two in your elementary school to help teach reading to younger children using computer software.
- Have girls teach word processing to other students.
- Start a program in which an older girl and boy meet weekly with a younger girl and boy to form a team in which they invent a remote-controlled device to move golf balls to places on a playing field. Teach the older children to help their younger partners develop their own solutions and give special encouragement to the younger girl.
- Arrange a lunch for girls taking Algebra I to meet and talk with older girls taking physics, calculus, and programming.
- Have middle-school girls give a computer workshop for elementary-school children.
- You and some of your senior girls can make an annual presentation at the junior high schools on the importance of math and science.
- Choose high-risk girls who are bright and capable but are showing signs of losing their way as your special assistants.
- Have older girls teach younger ones about equity issues.

Adult-to-Girls Strategies

- Invite a few girls who used to be students in your high school and are now majoring in math, science, or technology, and ask them to talk to girls about their college experiences.
- Hold a reception for girls and young women who graduated from school a few years ago and are now studying or working in technical fields.
- Ask your local chapter of the American Association of University Women (AAUW) to help you arrange a Career Shadowing Program, in which girls select female mentors on the basis of career interest and spend one day with her at work.

- Take advantage of Take Your Daughter to Work Day in late April every year by arranging career-shadowing opportunities for girls in technical fields.
- Set up a mentorship program for gifted seniors, enabling them to work with professionals in technical and mathematical fields during the day.
- Set up a summer mentorship program in which girls act as interns or assistants to women working in technical fields.
- If you teach an adult education computer course, ask the mothers to bring their daughters to class for one night. Serve refreshments.

Girl-to-Adult Strategies

- Have girls teach computer-illiterate teachers how to do word processing and Print Shop.
- Have girls encourage their mothers and aunts to take an adult education course in computers.

FOR PARENTS

Types of Parent Events

- Hold a workshop on gender equity for parents and girls on an evening or a Saturday morning.
- Have the principal moderate a panel discussion for parents on gender equity.
- Hold a session for parents on software selection and include gender equity considerations.
- Invite girls and adult women to a Women's Computer Night: Food, Fun, and Festivities. "Bring your mom, grandmother, or a special woman friend with you."
- Hold a daylong Mother-Daughter Colloquium on how schools can better serve girls. In small groups, have participants discuss individual aspects of girls' education and propose strategies for change.
- Do a presentation on gender equity at a PTA meeting.
- Hold a Saturday Computer Brunch for girls and an adult female of their choice, with food donated by local businesses. Plan enjoyable activities for girls and women to do at the computer, followed by brunch.
- Hold one- to five-part computer instruction sessions for mothers and daughters. Emphasize practical uses. Advertise them in the parent newsletter.
- Give a presentation on gender equity at the Parent University, a workshop series for parents meeting Saturdays.
- Hold a Parent-Daughter Night that focuses on the changing role of women in the workforce and the skills girls will need for jobs. Serve pizza for dinner to give parents one fewer thing to worry about.
- Speak about gender equity on Orientation Night for children who are new to the school and their parents.
- To introduce the school's new telescope to parents, have a Parents Science Night for training in how to use it, after which parents can borrow it at home for a few days (or rather, nights). Send along suggestions on how to use the telescope, including holding a Star Party for their daughters' friends to emphasize the social aspect of science. (Star Parties became the social hit of the season at this trainer's school!)

Parent Event Activities

- Invite parents of girls in your class to school in the evening. Have their daughter teach them how to use a spreadsheet.

- Hold a Mother-Daughter Share Night (or Father-Daughter Share Night) where girls can display their work. Invite the school board and administrators as well. Make a short speech about the importance of encouraging girls in this way.
- Open the school's computers to parents (and children) after school or on weekends on a regular basis. Have girls teach parents how to use the computers.
- Show a videotape, homemade or professional, about gender equity on a continuous-run basis near the food table.
- Encourage parents to come to an evening on equity by arranging for a drawing for a CD player.
- Have female students present their technical projects to parents. This can include a demonstration of telecommunications and videotapes produced by girls.
- Have a gender equity booth at a parent event at which you give handouts and talk to parents about their daughters' futures.
- Have a session at which parents brainstorm strategies to use at home to encourage their daughters in science, computers, or math.
- Design and conduct a survey of parents about equity concerns: which children have what toys and equipment, activities, discussions, career hopes, etc. Have girls enter and analyze the data. Share results with the parents.
- Have girls make presentations one evening to parents on their work in your subject.

Written Communications to Parents

- Arrange for equity-related facts and figures to be published in each issue of the newsletter for parents.
- Publish the names of all faculty and students active in equity activities in the parent newsletter.
- Send information on gender equity home to parents.
- If your equity work is featured in a local paper, send copies home to parents.
- Distribute handouts on gender equity at parent events. Sample handouts at parent workshop: the parent section of *The Neuter Computer*, or *Does Your Daughter Say "No, Thanks" to the Computer?* a list of books that portray females positively, copies of articles relating to gender equity.
- Distribute information to parents about jobs and salaries, stressing that jobs involving math, science, and technology tend to pay better than those that don't. Urge parents to discuss the information with their daughters and encourage daughters to enroll in advanced courses.
- Send articles home on sexism in toys, television, and child-rearing practices.
- Send personal notes to girls' parents urging them to encourage their daughters to persevere in your subject.

Other Parent Strategies

- Invite parents to accompany you and girls to Expanding Your Horizons conferences.
- Encourage parents to follow up their daughters' interest in your subject.
- Ask parents who have a home computer where it is kept. If the answer is "in a boy's bedroom," suggest they move it to more neutral territory.
- Urge parents not to accept as "natural" poor performance in your subject from their daughter, but rather to get her a tutor.
- Invite parents to a gender equity presentation with an invitation that reproduces recent newspaper headlines relating to women.
- Invite parents in technical occupations to participate in Career Day.

- Have girls produce a program booklet for a parent event using desktop publishing. Include a description of your gender equity efforts.
- Invite a few mothers to share in a presentation you make on gender equity to the PTA.

SCHOOL OR DISTRICT POLICIES

Evaluating and Purchasing Materials

- Have gender equity included on all evaluation forms for curriculum materials: textbooks, software, posters, etc.
- If you find that software or other educational materials are sexist, make it a district policy to tell the salesperson that this is the reason you are not buying the company's product. The company will get the message.

Personnel Hiring and Evaluation Procedures

- Be sure that at least one person who is sensitive to gender equity concerns is a member of the screening committee for a new principal.
- Have gender equity included in classroom observation and evaluation procedures and forms for current faculty.
- Ask job applicants to talk about what teaching techniques they use to encourage girls in math, science, and technology.
- As a performance evaluation component for math, science, and computer teachers, consider the extent to which girls and other underrepresented groups continue on to take advanced courses.

Data Strategies

- Analyze enrollment patterns by gender and race in upper-level classes as an annual procedure.
- Have all district outcome data analyzed by gender from now on, especially in math, science, and technology and any other gender-imbalanced curricular and extracurricular areas.
- Have an administrator do an equity survey in your building. Share the results with faculty and brainstorm strategies to correct problems that are revealed.

Policy Statements

- Include a statement on gender equity as a district goal: "To broaden gender and cultural representation of students in mathematically related courses" and "to increase the sensitivity of the school community to gender equity issues."
- Be sure your district has a solid sexual harassment policy. Develop it in consultation with students as well as faculty.
- If your district does not have a formal plan for increasing girls' representation in advanced math, science, and technology courses, write on and submit it to the school board for consideration.
- Print the text of Title IX on all district stationery to underline its commitment to equity: "It is the policy of the X Public Schools not to discriminate on the basis of sex, race, color, and national origin, in its educational programs, activities, or employment policies as required by Title IX of the 1972 Educational

Amendments. It is also the policy of X Public Schools not to discriminate on the basis of handicap in its educational programs and activities of employment as required by Section 504 of the Rehabilitation Act of 1973."

Planning Committees and Procedures

- Become a member of your district's technology initiative planning committee, or districtwide mathematics or science curriculum committees. Bring up gender equity regularly.
- Become a member of your district's textbook review committee. Make sure gender equity is considered each and every time.
- Speak with members of your district's math, science, and/or technology curriculum committees about the importance of gender equity action included in district policy procedures.
- Conduct a full-scale Title IX review.
- Adopt some of the recommendations of the American Association of University Women (AAUW) report, *Shortchanging Girls, Shortchanging America*.
- Develop a five-year plan for improvement in gender equity, with annual progress evaluations.

Other Policy Strategies

- Do not permit students to choose between industrial arts and home economics: require that all must take both.
- If your discipline program distributes merit awards to students who demonstrate positive traits, encourage teachers to nominate boys who show caring and kindness as well as girls who show curiosity and assertiveness.
- When you make a presentation to the school board on gender equity, be sure that supportive colleagues and/or parents are present to back you up.
- If your introductory computing class is optional and mostly boys sign up for it, make it mandatory.
- To prevent shy or nonassertive girls from dropping out of advanced math and science classes at the first sign of trouble, require that a teacher's signature be necessary to drop a class. Faced with such a request, a teacher can give extra help, attention, and encouragement to students who should be able to handle the class and thus prevent unnecessary dropouts.
- If the boys' basketball team is called the Tigers and girls' team is called the Lady Tigers or the Tigerettes, change the name of the girls' team to something less derivative and patronizing. (After all, the boys' team isn't called the Gentleman Tigers!)
- Write a gender equity component into all grant proposals in math, science, and technology.

RECRUITING GIRLS FOR ADVANCED COURSES OR CLUBS

Also refer to the "Mentoring" section, earlier in this appendix.

Informal Strategies

- Issue personal invitations. Urge your colleagues to do likewise.
- Recruit especially popular girls: others will follow their lead.

- Recruit girls for advanced classes in friendship groups, not individually, since few are willing to be the only girl in a class.
- Give lots of individual encouragement and praise. Strongly suggest girls take specific courses. Discuss career options with them.
- Write personal notes to girls about how they should take an advanced course next year.
- Personally recruit appropriate girls for the advanced courses you teach.
- When you see that a female student has not signed up for an advanced course you think she should be taking, do some one-on-one counseling with her.
- Have your student tutors make a special effort to keep girls involved in your subject.
- Have girls who are interested in taking an advanced course recruit their girlfriends to take the course with them.
- Have girls recruit their friends to attend extracurricular meetings and events with them.
- Allow girls who want to take the same section of a class together to do so.
- Don't wait for a girl to express interest in an advanced course; suggest it to her first.
- Invite other teachers to drop in at club meetings for a few minutes, accompanied by a couple of their female students.
- Be specific in describing what an after-school extracurricular activity will consist of.
- Offer after-school help to girls having trouble in your subject, and oppose an easy-out wish to drop your subject as soon as they can.
- Invite girls to attend club meetings in friendship pairs.
- Recruit especially girls with low self-esteem and girls who speak little English.
- Suggest that a group of girlfriends participate together in previously all-male activities such as remote-control cars and shooting hoops.
- Intensify female recruiting efforts just before course registration time.
- Tell girls that the computer club has a great deal of nongame software available for their use.
- Ask each female club member to bring one girlfriend to the next meeting.
- If there aren't enough girls at a club meeting, go out in the hall and invite some to come in and join you.
- Ask boys in your club to help recruit girls.
- Specifically invite girls to equity events who have ability but are showing signs of losing interest.
- Send a personal letter to each girl in accelerated math classes in middle school urging her to take more courses in your subject.
- Post announcements of materials and activities you would like to introduce girls to, to pique their interest.
- Ask girls what brings them to club meetings: what they are especially interested in, what they find especially satisfying. Use their answers to interest other girls in joining the club.
- Make up invitations to a club meeting and hand them out to girls randomly in the hallway. Be sure the invitations say "bring a friend."

Organized Strategies

- Invite students to lunch to talk about the activity you think they should be involved in.
- Go to your feeder schools and meet with faculty members and counselors. Describe why you need their help in encouraging girls to sign up for your course.
- Give an award certificate to the girl who is most helpful in encouraging girls to take advanced courses.
- Distribute the list of girls who attend club meetings to teachers, so they know whom to encourage to continue participating.
- Require that each boy who is a member of your after-school club bring one or more girls with him to the next meeting.

- Host a lunch for girls in advanced courses and younger ones who show promise. Serve pizza, with the following variations: (1) Have the host girls contact the invited girls personally; (2) have the invited girls' teachers urge them to attend the lunch; (3) have the host girls telephone the invited girls the night before the lunch to remind them to attend and to answer questions; (4) encourage invited girls to bring along a friend who might also be interested in the advanced courses.
- Start an equity club in your subject in which participants must bring a student of the opposite sex.
- Go to homeroom teachers and ask them to recommend appropriate girls to attend your club or event. Invite them personally.
- To have enough of an audience for a visiting speaker, prepare short printed information about her and what she will be speaking about. Make it sound interesting. Give it to girls ahead of time in homeroom period.
- With the members of your department, identify girls who are highly qualified to continue with advanced courses in your subject. Invite them to a meeting at which you urge them to continue.
- Take girls on a tour of the technology education or science classroom and demonstrate the equipment for them. Urge them to enroll.
- Change the course name from something technical to something more functional.
- Take pictures of girls participating in traditionally male classes and extracurricular activities, and show them to groups of girls as a recruiting tool. This is especially useful if you work at a vocational school and want to recruit girls for male-intensive vocational programs.

ROLE MODELS, VISITORS, AND SPEAKERS

Also refer to the "Field Trips" section, earlier in this appendix.

Whom to Invite

- Young women studying or working in technical fields, who are only a few years older than your students
- Current or retired college professors
- An Audubon Club member to build birdhouses with girls: good for spatial relations (and carpentry skills)
- Parents working in technical fields
- Women business owners or employees in technical fields
- A beauty contest winner who is a math, science, or engineering student or graduate
- A handsome young man to speak to girls about the importance of math, science, and technology for their futures
- Female scientists on Science Day
- Female mathematicians on Math Day
- Women in nontraditional careers, on Nontraditional Careers for Women Day
- Someone from a women's organization: historical, research, social service
- Someone from a professional association; ask for female speakers
- A female financial planner to discuss ways of paying for college
- Someone to discuss CAD-CAM (computer-aided design and manufacturing) career opportunities

Other Role Model Strategies

- Ask colleagues in your school and district, including school board members, for role model recommendations.

- When you give presentations on gender equity, ask participants for recommendations.
- Ask speakers to talk about any sexism they themselves have experienced and how it made them feel.
- Include boys as well as girls in the audience: they need to learn that women are competent professionals.
- When you have a nontraditional-career speaker in class, ask kids to guess how she earns her living.
- Invite speakers to come to your class during homeroom period, before they go to work, if this is more convenient for them.
- If you usually call the Chamber of Commerce for speakers and they usually send white males, tell them this is no longer acceptable.
- Establish and maintain a Hall of Success: photos and biographical summaries of, and visits by, female school graduates in technical fields. Keep in touch with graduates: ask them about their job history and tips of success to share with current students.

SCHEDULING AND RESOURCE ALLOCATION

Strategies for Overenthusiastic Boys

- Watch and pay attention.
- Hold a Girls Day and Boys Day.
- Have girls and boys alternate weeks.
- Have girls and boys take turns for prearranged amounts of time.
- Use a timer.
- Use a sign-up sheet that alternates boys and girls.
- Give all interested students a set number of coupons with which they can buy time with the resource. When they use up their supply they have to wait until the next coupon distribution.
- Reserve 50 percent of the resource for girls and 50 percent for boys. If there is also a problem with older students taking more than their fair share from younger ones, reserve by grade as well as sex.
- Have students sign up for slots and give them time in alphabetical order, not allowing anyone to have a second turn before everyone has had a first.
- Let boys use the resource on odd days and girls on even days.
- If boys in science lab groups use more than their fair share of the lab equipment, hand the equipment trays to girls and ask them to apportion the equipment among lab members.
- If you have better and worse equipment or machines in the same room, make sure girls and boys have equal access to the better ones.
- Halfway through the period have girls and boys switch.

Other Scheduling and Allocation Strategies

- Don't schedule an advanced math, science, or technology course in the same slot as a course that is popular with many girls.
- Don't schedule an extracurricular club or event in math, science, or technology at the same time as another club or event that is popular with many girls.
- If you don't currently have time for after-school clubs, convince the administration to extend the day somewhat to create a time slot for them.
- If there are too many after-school events or if budget cuts have eliminated the late bus, move yours to a lunchtime slot.

- If you feel too few girls would attend an academically challenging club after school, hold it in your free period for no more than eight to ten weeks. Ask supportive teachers if they would be willing to release a few girls from class once a week to attend.
- Hold special events for girls (and their parents) in the evening.
- If parents don't want daughters to stay late after school, schedule a breakfast club instead.
- Hold a lunchtime study group for girls and their friends and their friends' friends. Arrange for them to get their lunches from the teachers' line, which saves time and is prestigious.
- Open the computer room to free-time use after school.
- If a girl can't stay after school, find a time during the day to introduce her to the science, math, or computer activity you think she would like.
- If your school has a long lunch period, devote half of it to lunch and the rest to computers.
- If you are a computer teacher, invite girls who need little help from you to use the computers during your planning period.
- Use part of the study hall period for computer use.

SPREADING THE EQUITY WORD TO GIRLS AND BOYS

Verbally

- Start a girls' equity team or committee or discussion group.
- Give a workshop on gender equity in education and the labor market to girls.
- Hold a student assembly on gender equity.
- Hold discussion groups for girls.
- Invite speakers.
- Discuss current events relating to gender equity in class.
- Invite older women to speak about what sexism was like one or two generations ago.
- Speak with all eighth-grade girls about equity before they make high school course choices.
- Point out the pressures from peers, society, parents, television, etc., on girls *not* to achieve in math, science, and technology. Challenge them to resist the pressures.
- Hold a daylong World of Difference program addressing gender, race, and cultural issues. This is particularly useful in a culturally diverse school where some cultures are less supportive of women than others, and gives a chance to girls in those cultures to see how other women manage to pursue math and science.

Visually

- Tape equity cartoons and statistics up in the hallway. If you can't get local statistics, use national ones.
- Devote entire bulletin boards to women.
- Show students videos on gender equity in math, science, and technology.
- Create an Equity Wall, where teachers and students can put up articles, pictures, posters, or other items illustrating equity or inequity in education or the world at large.

Written

- Tape equity articles to the inside of the stall doors in the girls' bathrooms.
- Cut out newspaper articles relating to gender equity and give copies to students.

- Distribute labor market data showing what men and women earn in different occupations and about the extent of women's labor-force participation throughout their adult lives.
- Have a student reporter interview you about gender equity for an article in the school newspaper.
- Start a districtwide newsletter on equity for girls, written by girls in schools across the district.

SPREADING THE WORD TO COLLEAGUES

In Your School

Organize

- Start an equity team in your school, consisting of faculty, staff, and administrators at a minimum, and adding students, parents, and school board members if possible, to plan and carry out equity strategies.
- Hold a Saturday morning software review session for your colleagues. Speak to them about gender equity as an evaluation criterion. Include equity on the evaluation form they use.
- Hold a periodic discussion group with faculty members on gender equity topics.
- Take one minute at each faculty meeting to present an equity fact, point, or finding.
- If your faculty has organized study topics every year, suggest that some colleagues take equity for their topic.
- When new teachers are hired, you and your allies can have a discussion with them to ensure that they will assist with equity efforts in your school.
- If you are involved in a community career conference for students, tell teachers to nominate two-thirds girls to attend.

Advocate

- Specifically target guidance counselors with equity information so that they can be more active in encouraging girls to take more math, science, and technology.
- Talk about gender equity issues in politics, sports, and the workplace over lunch with your colleagues.
- Urge faculty members to nominate more girls for community program opportunities, such as those at local colleges.
- Speak often about gender equity to department chairs in math, science, and computing, and provide them with materials. Urge them to encourage their teachers to follow through.
- If a colleague of yours is taking a graduate education course, suggest that she or he do a project on gender equity. The same goes for you.
- Win over skeptical faculty members eventually by holding informal conversations with them over time about the need for and importance of gender equity action.
- If your school televises daily announcements, include a "guest editorial" segment and talk about gender equity.
- When faculty members make snide comments about equity, talk to them about their daughters.
- Offer yourself as a peer coach to observe and tally teacher-student interaction patterns.
- Remind teachers that they are in a better position to influence girls to continue on in math, science, or technology than counselors or administrators are.

Use Written Communications

- Write and distribute a simple newsletter periodically to your colleagues with their strategy ideas and achievements. This motivates them to *have* ideas and achievements, and to keep it up.

- Distribute copies of articles, preferably short ones, or reading lists to your colleagues.
- Write up and distribute minutes of equity team meetings to the entire faculty.
- Arrange for equity-related facts and figures to be published in each issue of the daily school announcements.
- Hand out gender equity materials at faculty meetings.
- Tape equity articles to the inside of the faculty bathroom door stalls.
- If you have a girls' equity team or committee or discussion group, they can do a bimonthly newsletter for faculty covering the equity issues the group discusses.

In Your District or Town

Teach

- Teach a gender equity workshop to all the principals in your district.
- Teach a multisession course on gender equity to faculty in your district, for in-service credit.
- Teach a gender equity workshop to math, science, and technology teachers at a lower grade level than yours.

Organize

- Start or join a districtwide gender equity task force.
- Include a time for gender equity in the district's conference day program and the "student-staff awareness day" program.
- Include an equity component in the classroom management workshop required for all new district teachers.
- Have bimonthly meetings with faculty who are active in gender equity activities in other schools, to share ideas and successes and to plan joint projects.

Advocate

- If your job includes observing classroom teaching, give teachers information on how to eliminate biased teacher-student interaction patterns, and follow up. If your job doesn't include this, get the information to someone whose job does.
- Ask administrators to foot the bill to send several faculty members to a nearby professional conference on gender equity.
- Offer your services to your superintendent as an internal gender equity consultant.
- Make an annual presentation to your school board on the status of gender equity in math, science, and computing in the district. Report changes from last year.
- Be a guest on a public-access cable television show to talk about gender equity in education. Variations: appear with girls, appear with parents. Another variation: videotape another presentation on gender equity and show that over public-access cable television.
- Convince your administration to award salary increase points to faculty who attend a gender equity workshop you teach.
- Arrange for public-service billboards to emphasize nontraditional career choices for young people.

Use Written Communications

- Circulate articles on gender equity to all the science, math, and computer teachers in your district.
- Feed equity information to a central office official who will send it out as a weekly bulletin to all district administrators.

- Write a short article on gender equity to be included in the newsletters distributed early in the fall to all town residents.
- Write a brief newsletter periodically for the math, science, and technology faculty in your district on equity topics and developments.

Use Other Strategies

- Make a videotape of yourself talking about gender equity. Have the film class splice in appropriate footage from other sources. Bring it with you to other schools or send it to be watched in your absence.
- Encourage your district administration to hire a national consultant for top-level gender equity staff development: the Family Math Program, Gender/Ethnic Expectations and Student Achievement (GESA), or others.

Outside Your District

Teach

- Teach a course on gender equity at a local college or university. If possible, arrange graduate credit for participants and a fee for yourself.
- Offer to teach a workshop on gender equity at schools in nearby districts.
- Present a concurrent session on gender equity at a local, statewide, regional, or national conference.
- List your name as a gender equity trainer with your state's Department of Education.
- Invite a state Department of Education representative to attend one of your gender equity workshops as a kind of "audition."
- Include attention to gender equity in all college or graduate courses you normally teach.
- Teach a summer minicourse on gender equity.
- Give a presentation to community groups that give scholarships to graduating seniors, to make sure they understand the importance (and the legal requirement) of gender-equitable scholarship awards.
- If you give in-service staff development sessions in your subject, include gender equity in each session.
- Bring a few girls along with you when you do an in-service session on gender equity. Have them speak about it from their point of view.

Organize

- Start or join an area-wide "gender equity in education" organization.

Advocate

- Bring up gender equity issues in all the education-related groups and committees you belong to.
- Talk to your friends about gender equity and encourage them to bring the issue up in the schools their daughters attend. Coordinate equity sessions for the next conference of your professional association.
- If a colleague of yours gives speeches in other schools because she or he has been named Teacher of the Year or some other reason, provide your colleague with equity information and suggest that it be incorporated into the speeches.

Use Written Communications

- Write an article on gender equity and submit it to one of your professional publications.
- Get an article written about your equity work in a local tabloid that is distributed free at supermarkets.
- Provide equity information to the math, science, and/or technology departments of your local college or university.

TEACHING TECHNIQUES

Classroom Interactions

- Make a conscious effort to call on girls no less than half the time, to give them as much time as boys to answer questions, and to ask them as many "how" and "why" questions as boys. Pay special attention to silent girls who rarely demand your attention.
- Make a conscious effort not to solve problems for girls when they need help, but rather to give them a clue that will enable them to solve the problems for themselves.
- Videotape teachers (including yourself) to enable yourselves to observe your own gender-related classroom behavior. You could videotape the students as well, and after a discussion of gender-biased behavior in the classroom ask them to watch the videotape with gender bias in mind.
- Ask students to tell you if you are calling on boys more than girls.
- Teach your students to recognize inadvertent inequitable behavior and help you eliminate it. You can even give them permission to hit you over the head—gently—when you let males do things for themselves but do things for females.
- To make sure you call on all students equally, two methods: (1) Write each child's name on an index card, three cards per child. Shuffle them and work your way down the stack to call on children; (2) write each child's name on a Popsicle stick, put them in a can, shake them up, and pull one out.
- Ask a colleague to observe you in class for gender bias in teacher-student interactions.
- Make a videotape with other faculty members on improved teaching styles after paying attention to gender-biased teacher-student interaction patterns.
- Be aware of girls who hang back in science lab; do not permit this behavior.
- Do not permit boys to make sexist comments or exhibit sexist behaviors in school. (You wouldn't permit racist talk or behavior, would you?)
- If you've been seating boys and girls alternately to keep boys in line, instead seat girls next to each other because they like helping each other figure things out. The boys will probably behave better than you expect, anyhow.
- If boys make fun of girls in class to the point that girls feel reluctant to ask or answer questions, ask a counselor to talk with the boys separately while you talk with the girls (or vice versa) about dealing with the problem.
- Think about whom you have in mind when you ask especially difficult questions. If it's boys, consciously ask these questions of girls.
- If some boys' obstreperous behavior to ask for help—calling out, waving their hands madly—discourages girls from asking for help, distribute red plastic cups to students and require that requests for help be expressed by placing the cup silently on top of the monitor or on the desk or lab table.
- Tell boys in your class you will not call on them unless they stop being so "grabby" in raising their hands.
- Ask a student to keep track of the number of girls and boys you call on, and to let you know if you call on boys disproportionately.

- Pay attention to where the girls are sitting. If they're clustered in the back of the room, change the seating order.

Appropriate Language

- Don't say "guys" to refer to girls.
- Help the sports coaches rewrite the regulations to avoid the generic "he."
- If you or your students use the supposedly generic "he" to refer to females as well as males, try using "she" once in a while to make the point that "he" really refers to males only.
- Encourage students to correct teachers who use the generic "he." "He or she," they should insist.
- Have girls tally the number of times boys interrupt them as they speak. Hold a discussion on the results.
- When speaking about technologically knowledgeable career people, deliberately alternate pronouns—she, then he.
- Don't refer to "the ladies in the office" but instead refer to them by name.
- At a faculty meeting, tally the number of times women are interrupted and the number of times men are. Announce your results.
- If girls tell you about sexist, demeaning, or exclusionary comments made in class by other teachers (such as, "You girls probably won't be interested in this"), talk to the teachers privately or ask an administrator to do so.

Chores and Tasks

- Ask your female student aides to do most of the technical tasks and your male student aides to do more of the paperwork.
- Make sure the female library aides work the computers half the time, while male library aides stamp due dates and reshelve books half the time.
- Insist that girls as well as boys learn to set up and use all electronic equipment: VCRs, video cameras, printers, scanners, and whatever else you have.
- Ask a girl to try out a new piece of classroom equipment or software for the first time.
- To help you become familiar with new software, ask girls to try the programs first and teach them to you.
- Ask girls to move equipment and carry things.
- If you find that mostly boys respond when you ask for volunteers for technical tasks, appoint helpers instead.

Other Teaching Technique Strategies

- Let girls see you using the computers—frustrations as well as successes, and how you go about solving problems.
- If you don't have enough computers for all the students, have girls and boys take turns (see "Scheduling and Resource Allocation").
- Teach your female student lab assistants or computer aides separately from the boys.
- If girls tell you they don't like your subject very much, explain to them why they need to learn it just the same. Emphasize how it will be useful to them in the future.
- Do not permit a photographer to pose a picture of a boy at a computer or lab table and a girl standing behind him.

- If you have an e-mail address at home, give it to your students. Some will prefer this private method of communicating with you and will learn to love the computer this way.
- If your female students are too comfortable with sexism, exaggerate it until they understand. If girls are reluctant to try to solve a problem, announce: "All girls out in the hallway until you come up with a solution." Put up pictures only of male scientists. Comment that women aren't smart enough to be scientists. When the girls finally object, hold a clarifying discussion.
- Ask girls what they think of the equity strategies you are carrying out: Do they work? Could others work better?
- If you discuss specific students at faculty meetings, check on how girls are doing in computers, math, or science.
- Especially if your classroom is windowless, liven it up with colorful posters and plants.
- If colleagues tell you they have taken students to conferences on careers in math, science, or technology, ask what proportion of the students they took were girls. They may not realize they took only boys.
- At the beginning of every grading period hand out an anonymous survey to your students about what they want and need from you. If many of the girls write back that you "talk too much and assume they know too much," work on improving.

BIBLIOGRAPHY

BOOKS AND ARTICLES

American Association for the Advancement of Science. *Benchmarks for Scientific Literacy*. New York: Oxford University Press, 1993.

Archbishop Fénelon. *The Education of a Daughter*. Bedford, MA: Applewood Books, 1847.

Avenida Ligaya Espaldon. "Public-Private Partnership for Education and Public Service: Toward a Globally Competitive Filipino Workforce." Paper presented at capstone lecture to the Board of Regents, Pamantasan Ng Lungsod Ng Maynila [University of the City of Manila], Manila, Philippines, November 10, 2006.

Bart, Jody. *Women Succeeding in the Sciences*. West Lafayette, IN: Purdue University Press, 2000.

"Bayer Facts of Science Education Survey, 2004." At www.bayerus.com/MSMS/news/facts.cfm?mode=detail&id=survey04.

Boyer, E. *High School: A Report on Secondary Education in America*. New York: Harper & Row, 1983.

Cavanagh, Sean. "As Test Date Looms, Educators Renewing Emphasis on Science." *Education Week*, March 30, 2005.

———. "Faking It Won't Make It in Science." *Education Week*, December 1, 2004.

Champagne, Audrey, and Leo Klopfer. "Research in Science Education: The Cognitive Psychology Perspective." In *Research Within Reach: Science Education*, edited by David Holdzkom and Pamela B. Lutz, 172–89. Charleston, WV: Research and Development Interpretive Service, Appalachia Educational Laboratory, 1984.

Coble, Charles, and Michael Allen. *Keeping America Competitive: Five Strategies to Improve Math and Science Education*. Education Commission of the States, July 2005.

"Constructivism Lesson Plan Format." At www.free-definition.com/Constructivism-%28pedagogical%29.html (August 21, 2005). [URL no longer active.—SGG]

Costa, Paul, Antonio Terracciano, and Robert McCrae. "Gender Differences in Personality Traits Across Cultures: Robust and Surprising Findings." *Journal of Personality and Social Psychology* 81, no. 2 (2001): 322–31.

Department of Elementary and Secondary Education. *Missouri's Proposed Academic Performance Standards (Draft)*. Jefferson City, MO: 1994.

———. *The Outstanding Schools Act: Senate Bill 380*. Jefferson City, MO: 1993.

Feingold, Alan. "Gender Differences in Personality: A Meta-analysis." *Psychological Bulletin* 116 (1994): 429–56.

Fitzgerald, Mary Ann, and Al Byers. "Teaching Strategies: A Rubric for Selecting Inquiry-Based Activities." At www.nsta.org/main/news/pdf/ss0209_22.pdf#search='definition%20of%20science%20inquiry' (accessed August 21, 2005).

Galley, Michelle. "Studies Suggest Science Education Neglected." *Education Week*, May 19, 2004.

Gurian, Michael. *Boys and Girls Learn Differently!* San Francisco: Jossey-Bass, 2001.

Hall, Tracey. "Differentiated Instruction Lesson Plan Format." At www.cast.org/publications/ncac/ncac_diffinstruc.html (accessed August 21, 2005).

International Association for the Evaluation of Educational Achievement. *Science Achievement in Seven Countries: A Preliminary Report*. Oxford: Pergamon, 1988.

Klein, Margrete, and F. James Rutherford, eds. *Science Education in Global Perspective: Lessons from Five Countries*. Boulder, CO: Westview Press, 1985.

Kober, Nancy. "EDTALK: What We Know About Science Teaching and Learning." Washington, DC: Council for Educational Development and Research, 2001. ERIC Documentation Reproduction Service No. ED361205.

Lapointe, Archie, Nancy Mead, and Gary Phillips. *A World of Differences: An International Assessment of Mathematics and Science*. Princeton, NJ: National Assessment of Educational Progress, Educational Testing Service, 1989.

Lewis, Michael. "Parents and Children: Sex Role Development." *School Review* 80 (1972): 229–40.

Moir, Anne, and David Jessel. *Brain Sex*. New York: Dell, 1990.

National Assessment of Educational Progress (NAEP). *The Third Assessment of Science, 1981–1982*. Denver, CO: 1983.

National Research Council. *National Science Education Standards*. Washington, DC: National Academy of Sciences, National Academies Press, 1996.

——. *National Science Education Standards (Update)*. Washington, DC: National Academy Press, 1995.

Pomerantz, Eva, Ellen Alterman, and Jill Saxon. "Making the Grade but Feeling Distressed: Gender Differences in Academic Performance and Internal Distress." *Journal of Educational Psychology* 94, no. 2 (2002): 396–404.

"Problem-Based Learning," at www.edtech.vt.edu/edtech/id/models/pbl.html (accessed August 21, 2005).

——. www.aug.edu/teacher_development/PBL/Elementary%20Units/Courtyard/Plants.htm (accessed September 13, 2005). [URL no longer active.—SGG]

Public Policy Institute of California. "High School Girls Now Outnumber Boys in Most Math and Science Classes," news release, March 5, 2005.

Randolph-Macon College. "Concept-Based, Differentiated Lesson Plan Template." At faculty.rmwc.edu/mentor_grant/Differentiated/lesson_template.htm (accessed September 13, 2005).

Rubin, Jeffrey Z., Frank J. Provenzano, and Zella Luria. "The Eye of the Beholder: Parents' Views on Sex of Newborns." *American Journal of Orthopsychiatry* 44 (1974): 512–19.

Rubin, Kate. "No Rest for the Best." *Minneapolis Star Tribune*, April 8, 2002, D3.

Rutherford, F. James, and Andrew Ahlgren. *Science for all Americans*. New York: Oxford University Press, 1990.

San Diego State University. "Inquiry-Oriented/Constructivist Lesson Plan Format." At edweb.sdsu.edu/Courses/EDTEC470/sections/F02-10/lesson_planning.htm (accessed September 13, 2005).

"SciMath Minnesota K–12 Science Framework, Best Practice, Science for All." At www.scimathmn.org/frameworks_math.htm (accessed June 24, 2004).

Seton Hall University. "Science Lesson Plan Format." At education.shu.edu/pt3grant/zinicola/lessonplanformat.html (accessed February 5, 2007).

Shaka, Farella L. "Translating Current Science Education Reform Efforts into Classroom Practices." Association for the Education of Teachers of Science conference proceedings, Southwest Missouri State University, 1997. At www.ed.psu.edu/ci/Journals/97pap6.htm.

Skolnick, Joan, Carol Langbort, and Lucille Day. *How to Encourage Girls in Math and Science*. Palo Alto, CA: Dale Seymour Publications, 1982.

Thomas, Julie, and Jon E. Pedersen. "Draw-a-Science-Teacher-Test: Pre-service Elementary Teachers' Perceptions of Classroom Experiences." Paper presented at the meeting of the National Association of Researchers in Science Teaching, San Diego, April 1998.

——. "When Do Science Teachers Learn to Teach? A Comparison of School Children's and Pre-service Teachers' Science Teacher Illustrations." Paper presented at the conference of the Association for the Education of Teachers of Science, 2001. At www2.tltc.ttu.edu/thomas/conference%20paper/2001/2001.htm.

"TIMSS 1999 Benchmarking Report." At isc.bc.edu/timss1999b/sciencebench_report/t99bscience_chap_3_4.html.

Yager, R., and J. Penick. "Resolving the Crisis in Science Education: Understanding Before Resolution." *Science Education* 71, no. 1 (1987): 49–55.

ONLINE SOURCES

Below is a short list of possible websites that offer age-appropriate science lessons and activities. By planning lessons that align with the research on how girls learn, teachers can begin to teach meaningful, relevant science that will motivate girls and that may improve both achievement in science and increase girls' interest in pursuing careers in the field.

Pre-primary and Primary

www.urbanext.uiuc.edu/SchoolsOnline/
essc.calumet.purdue.edu/classroom_Activites/preschool
www.primaryresources.co.uk/science/science.htm
www.enchantedlearning.com/categories/preschool.shtml
eduscapes.com/sessions/butter/primary.htm
physics.owu.edu/EducationWorkshops/

Intermediate

www.girlscoutssdi.org/site/forms/pdf/PG-0442-.pdf
www.girls-explore.com
teacher.scholastic.com/grade/grades35/index.htm
www.edhelper.com/Science.htm
www.sitesforteachers.com/
www.kinderstart.com/learningactivitiesandcrafts/earthscienceandnature.html
physics.owu.edu/EducationWorkshops/

Middle School

www.nap.edu/html/rtmss/indextitles.html
physics.owu.edu/EducationWorkshops/
www.learner.org/catalog/extras/activities/
www.pbs.org/teachersource/health_fitness/middle_anatomy.shtm
www.sciencefairprojects.biz/simple-middle-school-science-experiments.html

ABOUT THE AUTHOR

Susan Gibbs Goetz, EdD, is a former elementary-, middle-, and high-school science teacher who now brings her education and experience to bear on helping prepare others to do the same kind of work. She arrived at the College of St. Catherine in St. Paul, Minnesota, as an assistant, now associate, professor of science education in 1999, after serving for five years as an elementary-school principal. At St. Kate's, she also directs the undergraduate and graduate initial licensure programs, codirects the Center for Women, Science and Technology (CWST), has developed curriculum, and teaches in the recently created Science, Technology, Engineering and Mathematics (STEM) minor.

In addition, she teaches a core course, Global Search for Justice, in which she takes students to Namibia and South Africa. Goetz's interest in Africa springs from her work as a Fulbright scholar, which took her to Namibia to conduct research on the environment in the emerging democracy not long after it gained its independence from South Africa in 1990. Since 2002, she also has served on the Fulbright Association Science and Environment Task Force.

Among the many other academic and educational pursuits to which she devotes her time, talents, and abundant energy, Goetz is a mentor in a 3M-funded grant program that serves preservice teachers, student teachers, and first-year teachers in math and science. Also active on the lecture circuit, she has presented at numerous national and international conferences and published articles on her work in gender education and her work in STEM education.

Goetz earned Master of Arts (environmental science, 1981) and Doctor of Education (educational foundations, policy, and administration, 1994) degrees from the University of Michigan, where she also taught upper-level and graduate educational methods classes. A cum laude graduate of Purdue University (1976), she earned a bachelor's degree in ethology—a branch of zoology that involves the scientific study of animal behavior—from Purdue University and conducted field studies on a pack of wolves.